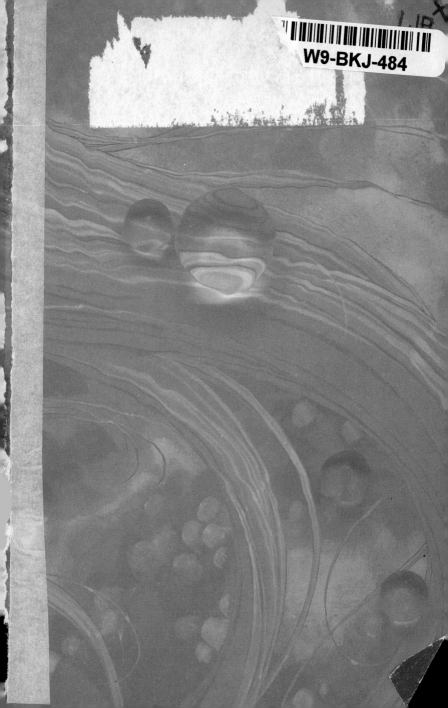

MUTSUMI MASUDA, C.B. CEBULSKI AND **KIA ASAMIYA**
Translation and Adaptation

LAURA JACKSON AND **YOKO KOBAYASHI**
Additional Translation

DAN NAKROSIS AND **DANO INK STUDIOS**
Retouch and Lettering

VANESSA SATONE
Designer

EVE GRANDT
Production Assistant

STEPHEN PAKULA
Production Manager

MIKE LACKEY
Director of Print Production

STEPHANIE SHALOFSKY
Vice President, Production

JOHN O'DONNELL
Publisher

CentralParkMedia.com
CpmPress.com

Dark Angel Book Three. Published by CPM Manga, a division of Central Park Media Corporation. Office of Publication – 250 West 57th Street, Suite 317, New York, NY 10107. Original Japanese Version "DARK ANGEL Volume 3" © 1994 Kia Asamiya. Originally published in Japan in 1994 by KADOKAWA SHOTEN PUBLISHING Co., Ltd., TOKYO. English version ©2000, 2001, 2004 Central Park Media Corporation. CPM Manga and logo are registered trademarks of Central Park Media Corporation. All rights reserved. Price per copy $9.99, price in Canada may vary. ISBN: 1-58664-927-2. Catalog number: CMX 62903MM. UPC: 7-19987-00623-2-00311. Printed in Canada.

World Peace Through Shared Popular Culture™

DARK ANGEL

BOOK THREE

CPM ®
MANGA
New York, New York

KIA ASAMIYA
Story and Art

CONTENTS

LEEN

The Phantom Saint of the Blue Dragon. Having recently assumed the mantle of Phantom Saint, Leen must deal with her newfound responsibilities, as well as defend against people that want her throne.

SHIKI

She is the dragon spirit who accompanies Leen. She is looking for the golden orb lost by the Phantom Saint, but has yet to find a clue.

CHARACTER PROFILES

GAN

He is one of the twelve dragon gods serving Leen. Despite his enormous stature and extraordinary strength, he is simple and pure of heart.

RAN

She is one of the twelve dragon gods serving Leen. She is always calm and faithful to Leen at all times.

NIE

Also known as the Black Dragon, she is one of the twelve dragon gods serving the Phantom Saint. She is annoyed when Mei, the former Phantom Saint, chooses Leen as his successor.

STORY SO FAR...

Dark is a young swordsman searching for his true destiny. Guided by his spirit helper Kyo, and by his own search for mastery of the arts of war, magic and moral action, Dark met many powerful opponents ready to test him and help him achieve his destiny as a Phantom Saint of the Red Phoenix. After battling these newfound adversaries, Dark walked off on his own, looking for more challenges to test his mettle against. But he is not the only Phantom Saint in the land. In this new adventure, Leen, the Phantom Saint of the Blue Dragon, has problems of her own. Someone wants her dead...and will stop at nothing until the job gets done.

THE LAND OF TOI
FF FSSS
FWOOOSHH

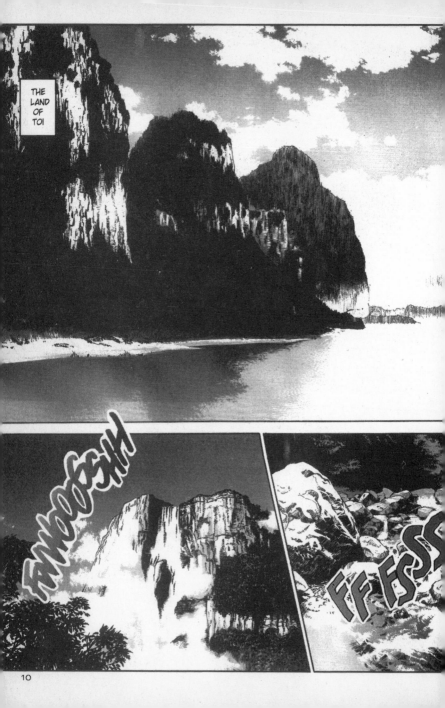

SSSSSHHHHHH

SSSSHHH
LEEN-
SAMA!

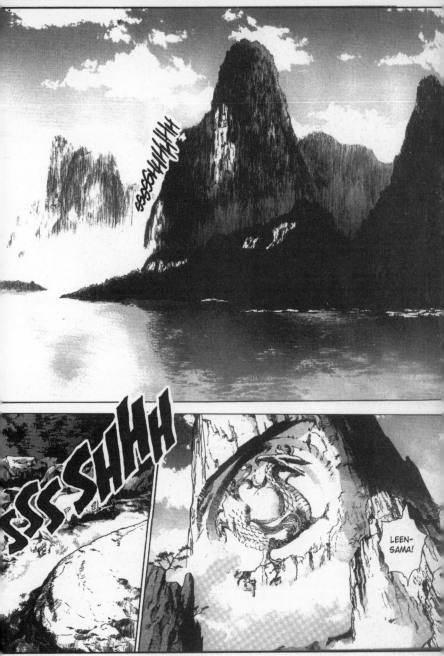

LEEN-SAMA!
LEEN-SAMA!
BLUE DRAGON PALACE.
SSSHHHHHHHH
LEEN-SAMA!
!
SSSSHHH
THAT VOICE...

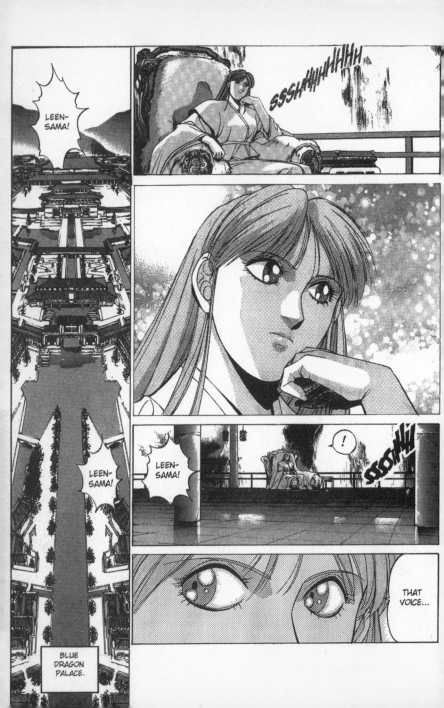

LEEN-SAMA!
IT'S BEEN A LONG TIME!
SHIKI?!
IS THAT YOU, SHIKI?!
YOU'VE FINALLY RETURNED!! WERE YOU SUCCESSFUL IN YOUR QUEST?
YES! I HAVE NEWS REGARDING THE ORB OF GOLD!
THAT'S WONDERFUL, MY LITTLE DRAGON SPIRIT.
COME AND TELL ME ALL ABOUT IT.

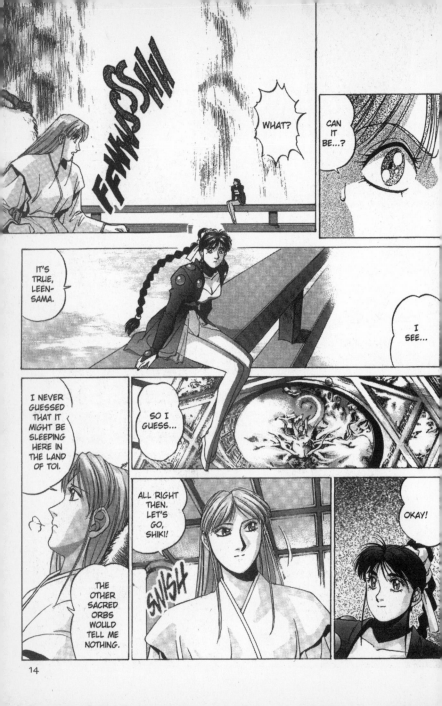

WHAT?

CAN IT BE...?

IT'S TRUE, LEEN-SAMA.

I SEE...

I NEVER GUESSED THAT IT MIGHT BE SLEEPING HERE IN THE LAND OF TOI.

SO I GUESS...

ALL RIGHT THEN. LET'S GO, SHIKI!

OKAY!

THE OTHER SACRED ORBS WOULD TELL ME NOTHING.

SNISH

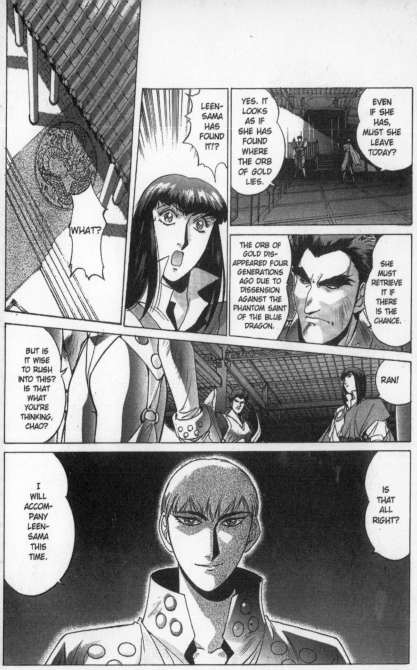

LEEN-SAMA HAS FOUND IT!?

YES. IT LOOKS AS IF SHE HAS FOUND WHERE THE ORB OF GOLD LIES.

EVEN IF SHE HAS, MUST SHE LEAVE TODAY?

WHAT?

THE ORB OF GOLD DIS-APPEARED FOUR GENERATIONS AGO DUE TO DISSENSION AGAINST THE PHANTOM SAINT OF THE BLUE DRAGON.

SHE MUST RETRIEVE IT IF THERE IS THE CHANCE.

BUT IS IT WISE TO RUSH INTO THIS? IS THAT WHAT YOU'RE THINKING, CHAO?

RAN!

I WILL ACCOMPANY LEEN-SAMA THIS TIME.

IS THAT ALL RIGHT?

15

CHAO...I THINK YOU SHOULD TAKE A BREAK. YOU'RE NOT THE ONLY ONE WHO CAN PROTECT LEEN-SAMA.
WHAT DO YOU MEAN?!
OKAY.
IT'S DECIDED THEN. YES?
BUT...

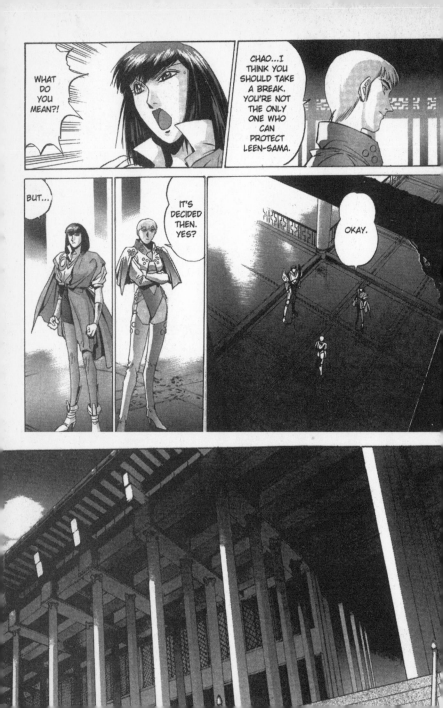

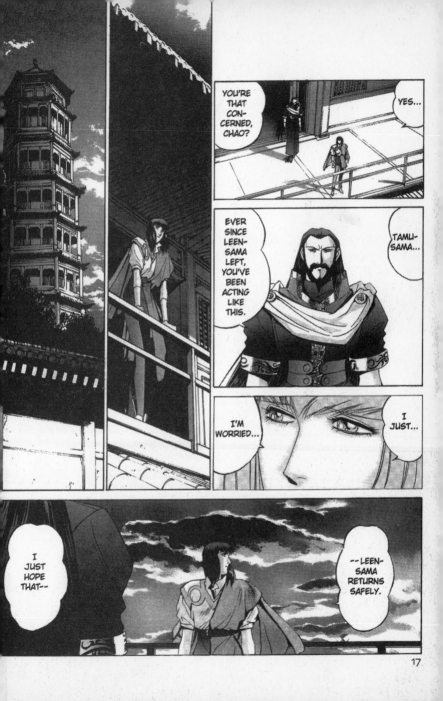

YOU'RE THAT CONCERNED, CHAO?

YES...

EVER SINCE LEEN-SAMA LEFT, YOU'VE BEEN ACTING LIKE THIS.

TAMU-SAMA...

I'M WORRIED...

I JUST...

I JUST HOPE THAT--

--LEEN-SAMA RETURNS SAFELY.

SHHSHHSHH
SSHH
SSHH
SSHH
SSHH

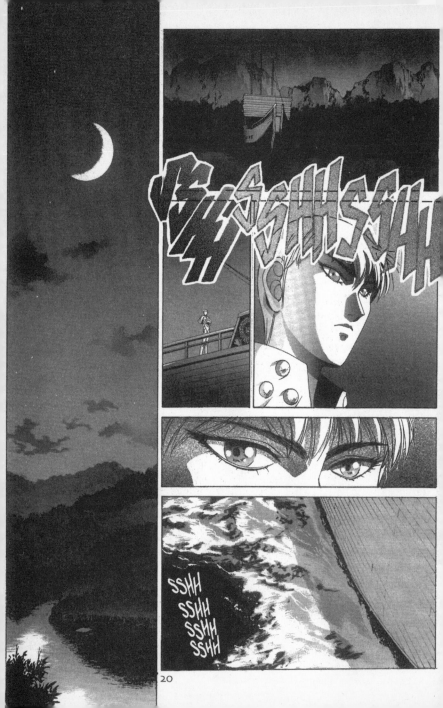

SO WHERE IS THIS PLACE WHERE THE ORB OF GOLD MIGHT BE FOUND?
WELL, LEEN-SAMA...
IT'S ABOUT 130 LI* FROM THE BLUE DRAGON PALACE.
THE ORB OF GOLD IS SUPPOSED TO BE IN THE VALLEY ON THE OUTSKIRTS OF THE VILLAGE OF SHIGO.
I SEE.

*ONE LI IS 3.93 KM = 1.60 MILES

I JUST RECENTLY HEARD THAT GOLDEN LIGHT EMANATES FROM THE VALLEY, ILLUMINATING THE SKY EVERY FIFTEEN KYOTEN.*
THIS LIGHT MUST BE--

* ONE KYOTEN = THREE DAYS

--THE ORB OF GOLD.
YES!

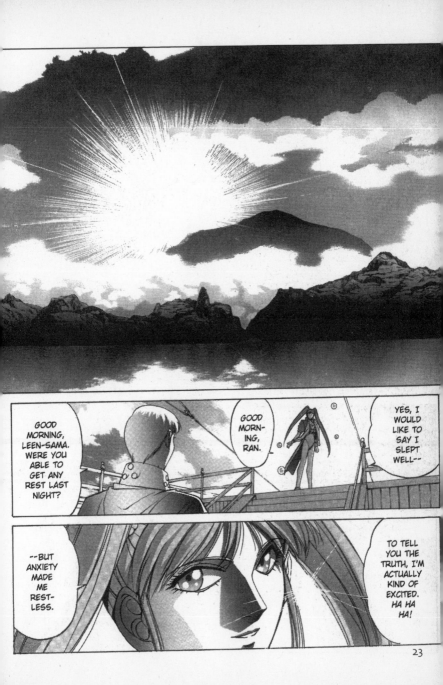

GOOD MORNING, LEEN-SAMA. WERE YOU ABLE TO GET ANY REST LAST NIGHT?

GOOD MORNING, RAN.

YES, I WOULD LIKE TO SAY I SLEPT WELL--

--BUT ANXIETY MADE ME RESTLESS.

TO TELL YOU THE TRUTH, I'M ACTUALLY KIND OF EXCITED. HA HA HA!

HAVE YOU SEEN SHIKI?
SHE'S STILL ASLEEP. SHE'S EX-HAUSTED.
ZZZZZZZZZ
IT'S UNDER-STANDABLE AS SHE HAS JUST RETURNED FROM A THIRTY GOTEN JOURNEY. AND NOW TO TRAVEL AGAIN SO SOON...
HMMM!
RAN-SAMA, WE WILL REACH THE SHIGO SHORE IN APPROX-IMATELY FIFTEEN KEI.*
I UNDERSTAND. KEEP OUR PRESENT SPEED. INFORM ME WHEN WE ARE ONE KEI FROM PORT.
YES, SIR!
THE RIVER SMELLS LOVELY IN THE MORNING. SOAKING IN THIS AIR, I FEEL AS IF MY ENTIRE BODY IS BEING CLEANSED.
MMM

*ONE KEI IS FIVE MINUTES, FIFTEEN KEI IS SEVENTY-FIVE MINUTES.

...
LEEN-SAMA...
HUH?
plop

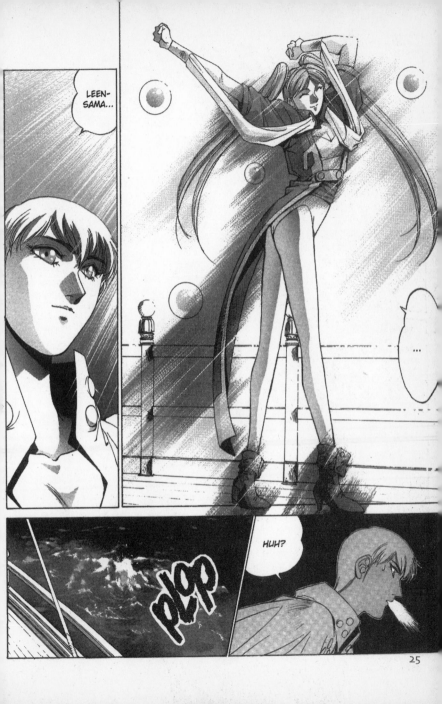

YEARGH!
SPLOOOSH
MAN YOUR STATIONS! I WANT A STATUS REPORT!
YES, SIR!
WHAT?
RATTLE
UGH!
WHAT?!

RAN-SAMA, PLEASE ABANDON THE SHIP! FOR YOUR SAFETY!!
!!
THWOOM
CAN WE MAKE IT THROUGH THIS?
LEEN-SAMA!
LEEN-SAMA! THE SHIP!
SHIKI!

KRRSH
CRRAAK
YAAHH!
BLUB! BLUB!
BLUB!
SCHWOO OOOOPPP

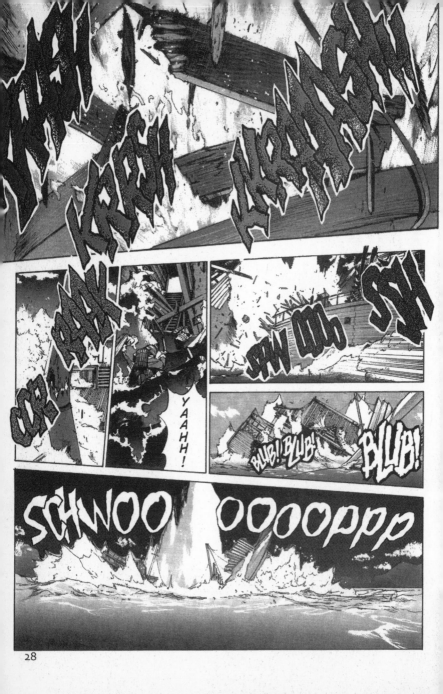

C CRRAACCK
KKR RAASSH
VWOOOOSH
VWOOOOOSH

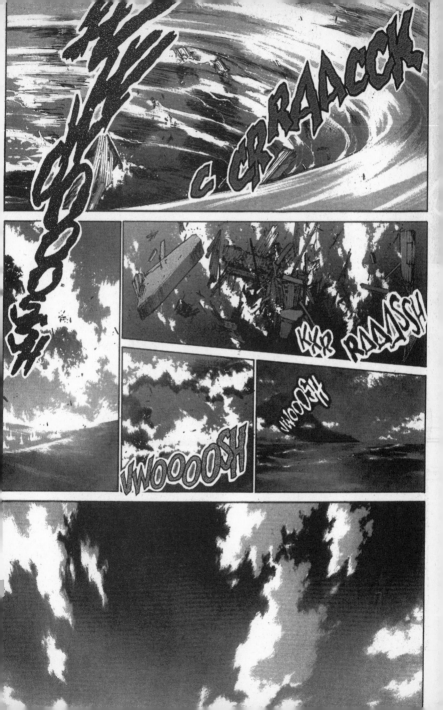

SPLISH
SPWASH

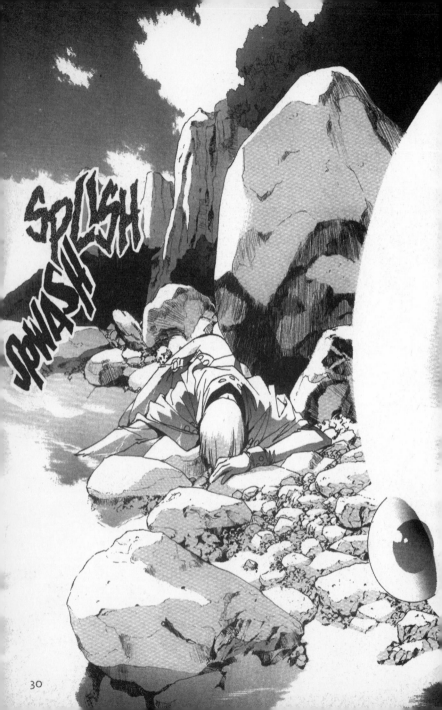

EVEN WITHOUT THE ORB OF GOLD--
--THE OTHERS PROTECTED THE PHANTOM SAINT.
IMPRESSIVE.
HA HA HA HA!
...
... UH...
HUH?!
SHOCK!
LEEN-SAMA!

I SEE. THE ORBS OF EARTH, WATER, FIRE AND WIND--
--PRO-TECTED LEEN-SAMA.
drip
BUT EVERY-ONE ELSE...
THEIR BODIES ARE NOT EVEN FLOATING UP. DAMN.

THAT WAS SOME SORT OF EXPLOSION OR...THE SHIP WENT DOWN QUICKLY, MUCH FASTER THAN IT SHOULD HAVE...

IT'S GOT TO BE...

SOMEONE PLANNED THIS...

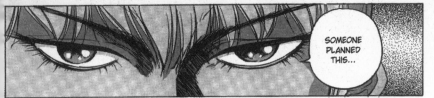

UGH...

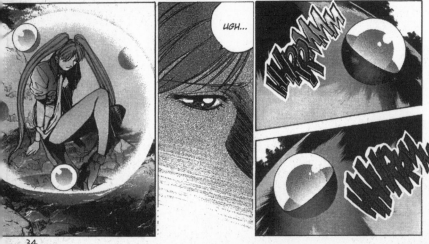

VHRRAMMM

VHRRAMM

AHH! I'M...
LEEN-SAMA!
I WAS WORRIED ABOUT YOU.
RAN! YOU'RE UNHURT. AND THE OTHERS?
THEY'RE...
I SEE. EVERY-ONE ELSE IS...
FWOOSH

LEEN-SAMA!
LEEN-SAMA! YOU'RE ALL RIGHT!!
SHIKI, I SEE YOU'VE SURVIVED AS WELL.
SPOK
YES. BUT I WAS STUCK IN THE WATER.
HEH HEH HEH!
I CAN SEE. YOU'RE ALL WET.
...
IS THAT SO? EVERY-ONE ELSE IS...

WE WILL HAVE TO CONDUCT THE DRAGON WATER FUNERALS, BUT...
WE SHOULD TRY TO CONTACT THE BLUE DRAGON PALACE TO RECOVER THEIR BODIES, IF THAT'S POSSIBLE.
YES...
RAN, CAN YOU MENTALLY CONTACT THEM?
I THINK... I STILL HAVE THE POWER FOR THAT.
I UNDERSTAND.
SHIKI, HOW LONG WILL IT TAKE TO GET TO THE VALLEY FROM HERE?
IF WE WALK, IT MAY TAKE ABOUT ONE KYOTEN.
IT WOULD BE FASTER IF WE JUST GO BY OURSELVES RATHER THAN WAIT FOR THE OTHERS TO ARRIVE FROM THE PALACE.
YES.

HMMM...

LEEN-SAMA, I'VE CONTACTED THEM.

IT WILL TAKE THEM ABOUT THREE KYOTEN* TO GET HERE.

*ONE KYOTEN IS THREE DAYS, THREE KYOTEN IS NINE DAYS.

THANK YOU. WE SHOULD REST A WHILE BEFORE WE DEPART.

BUT THE PEOPLE WHO ATTACKED US...

WHAT DO THEY WANT?!

YES!

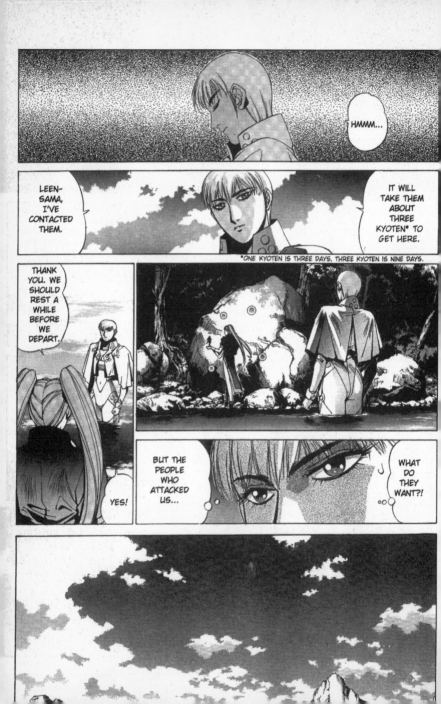

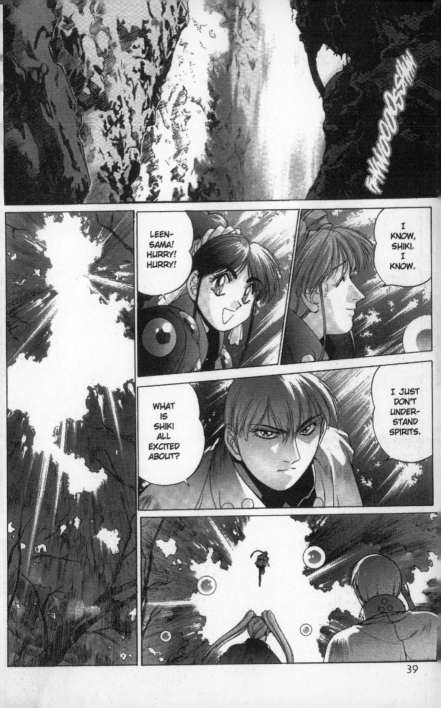

FWOOOO-SHH

LEEN-SAMA! HURRY! HURRY!

I KNOW, SHIKI. I KNOW.

WHAT IS SHIKI ALL EXCITED ABOUT?

I JUST DON'T UNDERSTAND SPIRITS.

THIS IS JUST BREATH-TAKING!
I TOLD YOU! I FOUND IT BY CHANCE LAST TIME.
I REALLY WANTED TO SHOW YOU THIS, LEEN-SAMA!
IS SOME-THING WRONG?
SHIKI, DON'T TELL ME WE CAME ALL THIS WAY JUST FOR THIS!
PHEW!

HA HA HA!
WHY, YOU LITTLE...
HMPH!

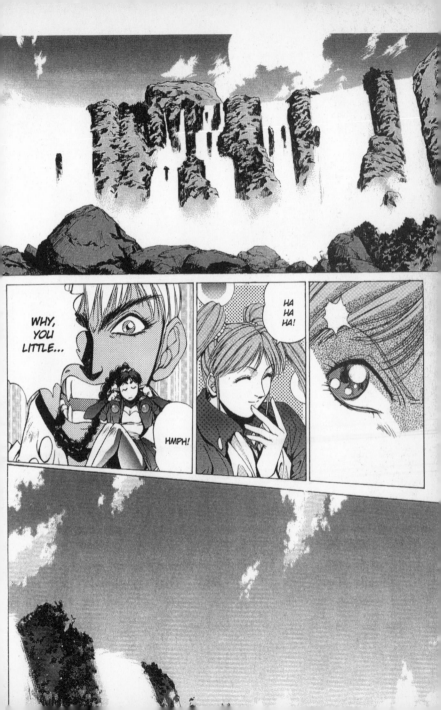

BWOOOOOM
WHAT!?
LEEN-SAMA!

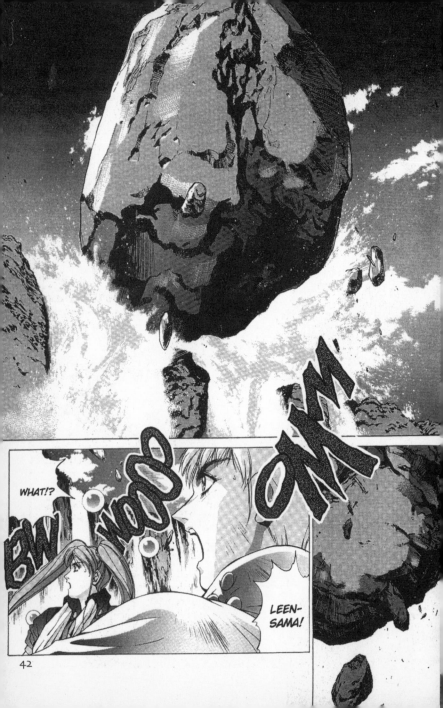

SHH HHH
SSSS
FFSSS
I...I DON'T KNOW.
SHIKI! DO BOULDERS USUALLY FALL AS FREELY AS THE WATER HERE?
I UNDER-STAND.
LEEN-SAMA, WE SHOULD GO. QUICKLY! I DON'T ADVISE REMAINING HERE.
WHO THE HELL WOULD ATTACK LEEN-SAMA?
WHO?

I WOULD!!

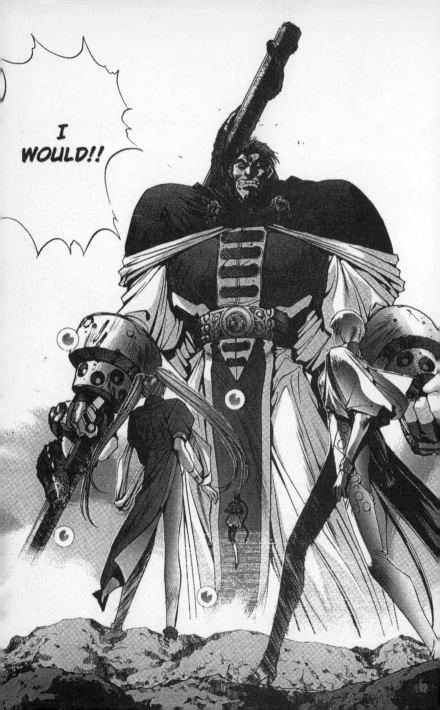

WHY?
GAN! YOU'RE SUPPOSED TO BE AT THE BLUE DRAGON PALACE!
G... GAN?
GRIN
WHY?
SWISHH
HERE'S WHY!

KERRRR
SSHHH
THWOK
GAN!! WHAT ARE YOU DOING?!
ARRRGH!
LEEN-SAMA, IT IS HERE THAT YOU WILL DIE!

HEH HEH. IT IS NOT I ALONE.
!?
ONE OF THE TWELVE WARRIORS OF THE DIVINE DRAGON IS TRYING TO TAKE LEEN-SAMA'S LIFE?! ARE YOU CRAZY?!
!!
RAN!! YOU ARE ALSO ONE OF THE TWELVE WARRIORS OF THE DIVINE DRAGON. ONE OF THE ELITE BLUE DRAGON WARRIORS CAN PROTECT LEEN-SAMA ALL BY HERSELF, NO?!
HA HA HA HA HA HA!!

RAN!
LEEN-SAMA, STAY BACK!
HIYYYAAAHHH!!
CRANG

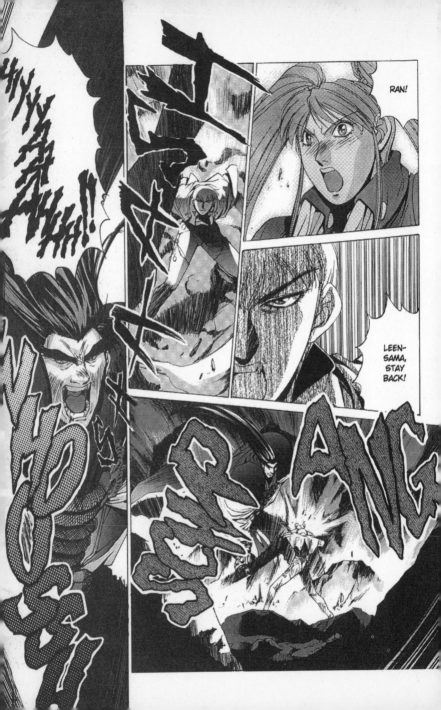

RAN!

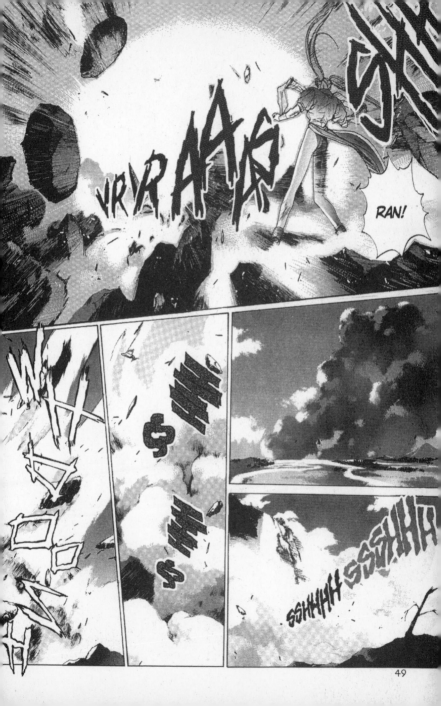

FSSSHHH
RAN!
RAN!
PWOOSH
SHIKI?!
LEEN-SAMA, DON'T GO IN THERE! LEAVE HERE QUICKLY!
DON'T BE FOOLISH! LEAVE?! WHAT ABOUT RAN?!?!
!!
HUH?

WHERE'S RAN...?
ALL IT TOOK WAS ONE BLOW. EASIER THAN I EXPECTED ACTUALLY. HA HA HA.
FWOOOOOSSHH
SHE WAS NOT WORTHY OF BEING A WARRIOR OF THE DIVINE DRAGON. HA!
THOK

!!
EH?
THAT'S...
DRAGON WIND?

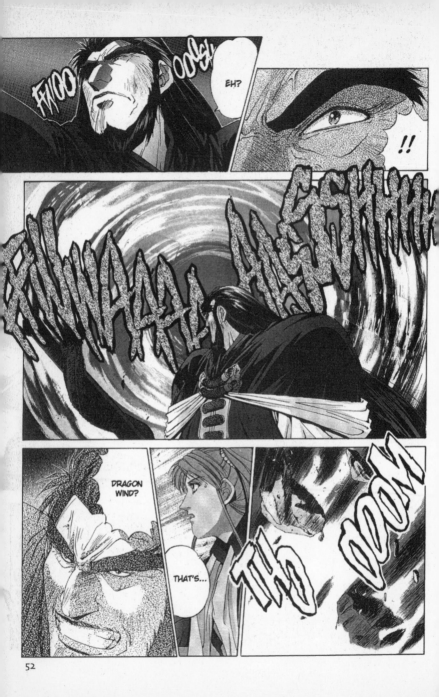

WHOOSH
ARGH!

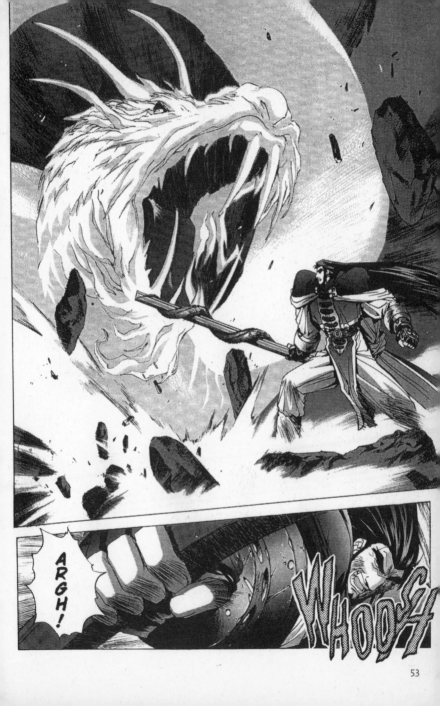

HRMPH...
I WILL NOT DIE BEFORE DISCOVERING THE TRUTH.
ANSWER ME! WHO IS IT THAT SEEKS TO END LEEN-SAMA'S LIFE?
WHAT WERE YOU SAYING, GAN?!
A WARRIOR OF THE DIVINE DRAGON DOES NOT DIE THAT EASILY!

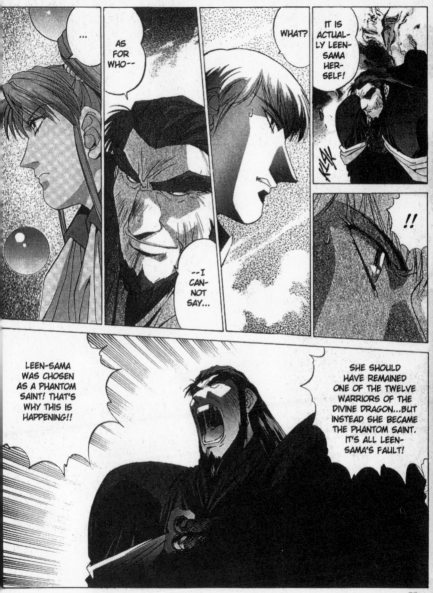

... AS FOR WHO-- WHAT? IT IS ACTUALLY LEEN-SAMA HERSELF!

KLAK

--I CANNOT SAY...

!!

LEEN-SAMA WAS CHOSEN AS A PHANTOM SAINT! THAT'S WHY THIS IS HAPPENING!!

SHE SHOULD HAVE REMAINED ONE OF THE TWELVE WARRIORS OF THE DIVINE DRAGON...BUT INSTEAD SHE BECAME THE PHANTOM SAINT. IT'S ALL LEEN-SAMA'S FAULT!

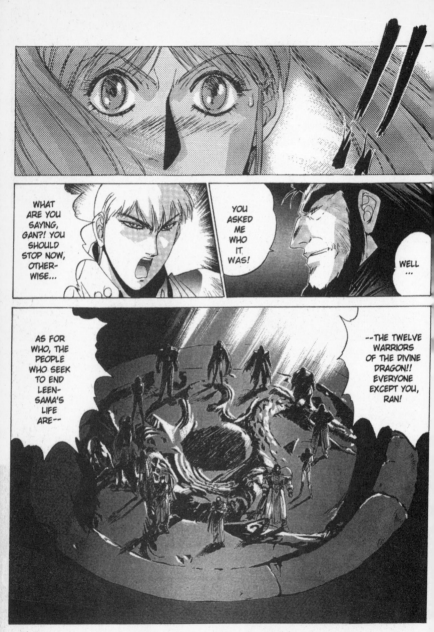

WHAT ARE YOU SAYING, GAN?! YOU SHOULD STOP NOW, OTHER-WISE...

YOU ASKED ME WHO IT WAS!

WELL...

AS FOR WHO, THE PEOPLE WHO SEEK TO END LEEN-SAMA'S LIFE ARE--

--THE TWELVE WARRIORS OF THE DIVINE DRAGON!! EVERYONE EXCEPT YOU, RAN!

...
NO, IT'S A LIE! YOU'RE LYING!
THAT'S... THAT'S RIDICULOUS!
YOU WILL SEE THE TRUTH WITH YOUR OWN EYES!
YOU WILL SOON FIND OUT WHETHER OR NOT I SPEAK THE TRUTH!

WHOO
OOSHH!!
IT'S BECOMING NIGHT!
THIS IS...
WOOOSH
DARKNESS IS ENGULFING THE SKY...

THERE'S ONLY ONE PERSON WHO COULD DO THIS!
ONE OF THE TWELVE WARRIORS, YOH OF SHO-KURYU.
UGHH!
RAN!!
DON'T EVEN THINK OF MOVING!
AHH!
UGH!
COME ONE STEP CLOSER AND I'LL BREAK HER NECK! HA HA HA HA!

SPL
GAN! CONTROL YOUR-SELF!
!?
PWOOSH
A WATER CHAMBER!
LEEN-SAMA!
DAMN...

DO YOU KNOW WHO IS THE ONE PERSON THAT CAN DO THAT, RAN?
ANOTHER OF THE TWELVE WARRIORS, KEI OF OURYU!!
IMPOS-SIBLE! ARE YOU SAYING THAT...
HA HA HA. EVEN THE PHANTOM SAINT CANNOT DEFEAT THE COMBINED MIGHT OF THE TWELVE WARRIORS OF THE DIVINE DRAGON!
...
LEEN-SAMA!
LEEN-SAMA!
KEI! TAKE LEEN-SAMA TO SEE THE BOSS!!

FWAA AASHH
LEEN-SAMA!!
SSHHOOOOOSSH

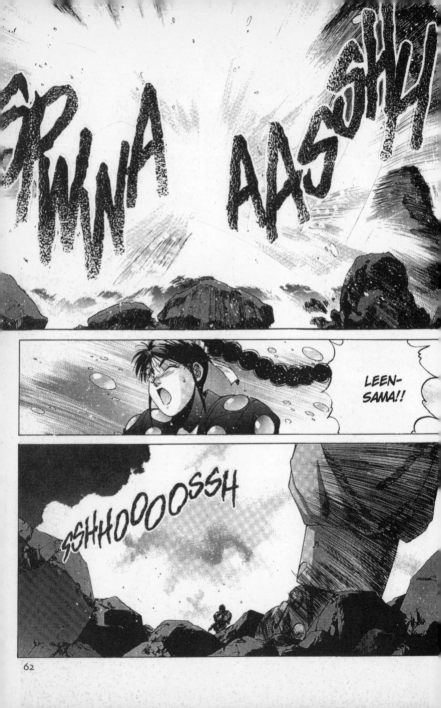

GAN! WHAT DO YOU PLAN TO DO WITH LEEN-SAMA?!
HEH!
POK
UHH...
NK
THO
UGH!
AM I FINISHED HERE, BLACK DRAGON?
FWOOOO OO OOSSHHH
YES, GAN. YOU CAN COME BACK NOW...
YES...

WHHOOOSH!
SPLASH
SSSH
BLUB BLUB!

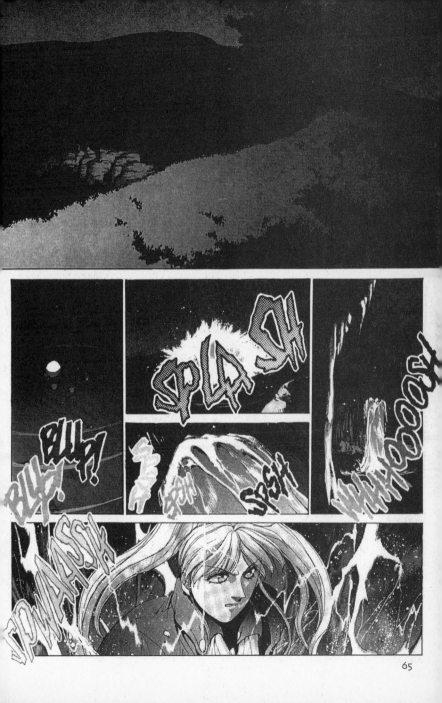

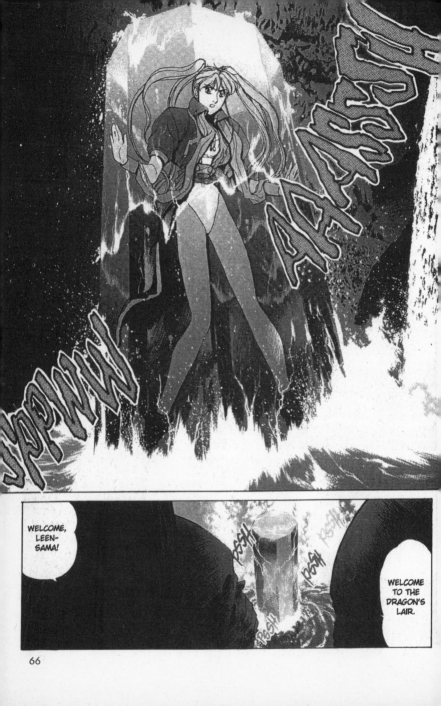

WELCOME, LEEN-SAMA!

WELCOME TO THE DRAGON'S LAIR.

66

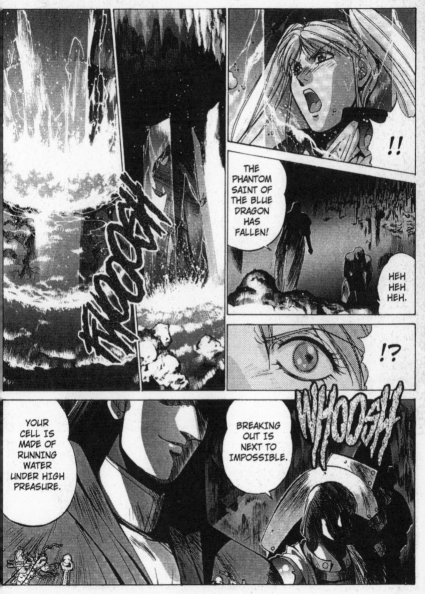

WHOOSH!!

!!

THE PHANTOM SAINT OF THE BLUE DRAGON HAS FALLEN!

HEH HEH HEH.

!?

YOUR CELL IS MADE OF RUNNING WATER UNDER HIGH PREASURE.

BREAKING OUT IS NEXT TO IMPOSSIBLE.

WHOOSH

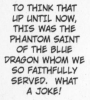

TO THINK THAT UP UNTIL NOW, THIS WAS THE PHANTOM SAINT OF THE BLUE DRAGON WHOM WE SO FAITHFULLY SERVED. WHAT A JOKE!

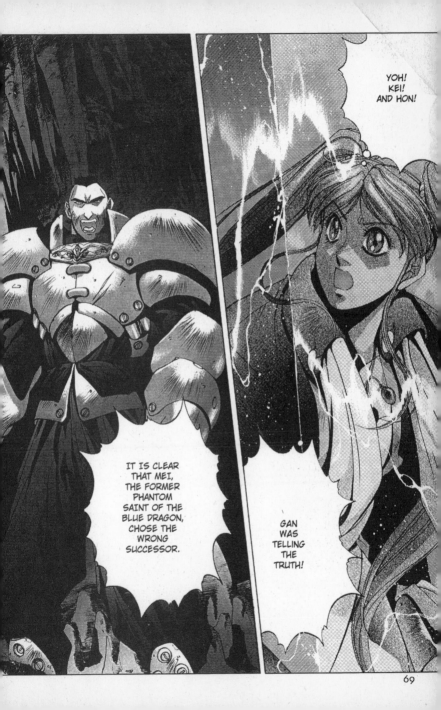

YOH!
KEI!
AND HON!

IT IS CLEAR
THAT MEI,
THE FORMER
PHANTOM
SAINT OF THE
BLUE DRAGON,
CHOSE THE
WRONG
SUCCESSOR.

GAN
WAS
TELLING
THE
TRUTH!

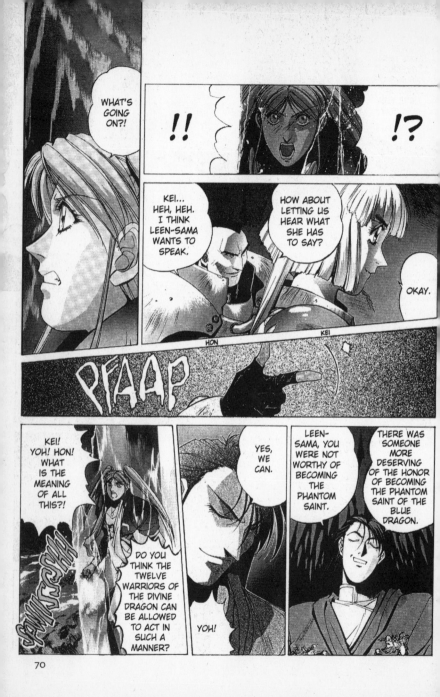

WHAT'S GOING ON?!

!!

!?

KEI... HEH, HEH. I THINK LEEN-SAMA WANTS TO SPEAK.

HOW ABOUT LETTING US HEAR WHAT SHE HAS TO SAY?

OKAY.

HON

KEI

PFAAP

KEI! YOH! HON! WHAT IS THE MEANING OF ALL THIS?!

DO YOU THINK THE TWELVE WARRIORS OF THE DIVINE DRAGON CAN BE ALLOWED TO ACT IN SUCH A MANNER?

YES, WE CAN.

YOH!

LEEN-SAMA, YOU WERE NOT WORTHY OF BECOMING THE PHANTOM SAINT.

THERE WAS SOMEONE MORE DESERVING OF THE HONOR OF BECOMING THE PHANTOM SAINT OF THE BLUE DRAGON.

YOU CAME HERE SEEKING THE ORB OF GOLD, BUT HERE YOU WILL DIE!
WHAT A PITY! AND YOU'VE ONLY BEEN PHANTOM SAINT FOR SUCH A SHORT TIME, TOO.
WHAT?
A NEW PHANTOM SAINT WILL TAKE YOUR PLACE NOW, LEEN-SAMA...
A PHANTOM SAINT WITH POWER!
WHO?
WHO COULD HAVE PLANNED THIS?
SHOOOOSH!!
I BELIEVE YOU KNOW THE PERSON STANDING BEHIND YOU.
BE-HIND ME...?

!!
THAT'S RIGHT, LEEN-SAMA. IT IS I!

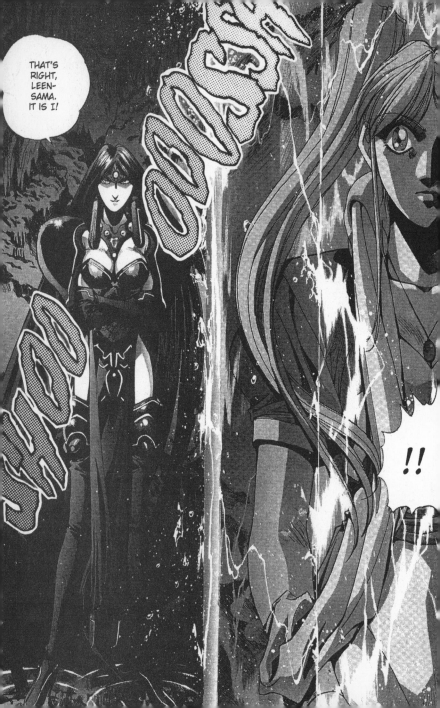

UGGH!
DO IT RAN!
MY SECRET SKILL!
WSSSHHH

YOU!
NIE, THE BLACK DRAGON!
I WILL TAKE YOUR PLACE AS PHANTOM SAINT! HA HA HA!
WHY?! YOU AGREED TO MY BECOMING THE PHANTOM SAINT.
YOU ARE BETRAYING MEI-SAMA, THE FORMER PHANTOM SAINT!
AT THAT TIME, I HAD TO AGREE IN FRONT OF MEI-SAMA,
BUT...
I COULD NEVER FORGIVE THE FACT THAT SOMEONE WITH LESS POWER THAN ME BECAME PHANTOM SAINT.
LEEN-SAMA!
...

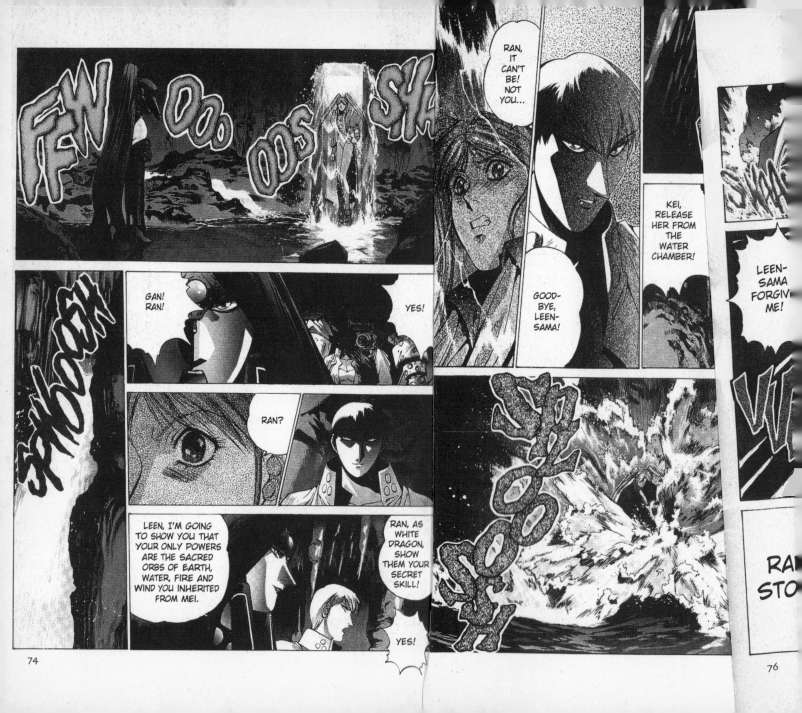

FFW OOO OOS SYA

FSHOOOOH

GAN! RAN!

YES!

RAN?

LEEN, I'M GOING TO SHOW YOU THAT YOUR ONLY POWERS ARE THE SACRED ORBS OF EARTH, WATER, FIRE AND WIND YOU INHERITED FROM MEI.

RAN, AS WHITE DRAGON, SHOW THEM YOUR SECRET SKILL!

YES!

RAN, IT CAN'T BE! NOT YOU...

KEI, RELEASE HER FROM THE WATER CHAMBER!

GOOD-BYE, LEEN-SAMA!

LEEN-SAMA FORGIVE ME!

RA STO

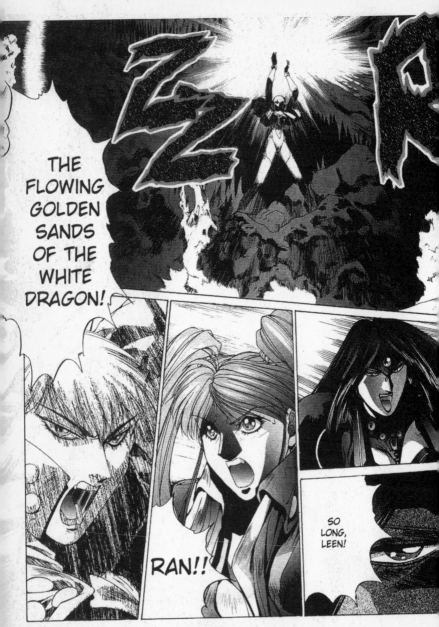

THE FLOWING GOLDEN SANDS OF THE WHITE DRAGON!

RAN!!

SO LONG, LEEN!

HA HA
HA HA
HA HA!

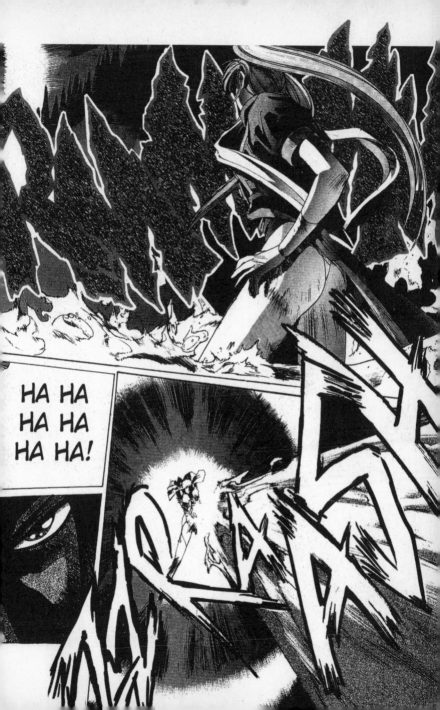

WHOOOSH
ZRAAP
!!
BWOOOOSH
SHRASH

...
THANK YOU.
GOOD JOB, RAN!
~SIGH~
THANKS TO RAN'S GOLDEN SANDS...
LEEN CAME HERE LOOKING FOR THE ORB OF GOLD. SHE NEVER DREAMED SOMETHING LIKE THIS WOULD HAPPEN.

HA HA HA HA!
SHE'S BECOME A GOLDEN STAUE HERSELF!!

YOU WILL SHINE BEAUTIFULLY AND EVERYONE IN THE PALACE WILL BE PLEASED.
HEE HEE. SHOULD I PUT YOU IN THE MAIN HALL OF THE BLUE DRAGON PALACE?

HEH!
KEI! RELEASE THE FOUR SACRED ORBS!
AL... ALL RIGHT.

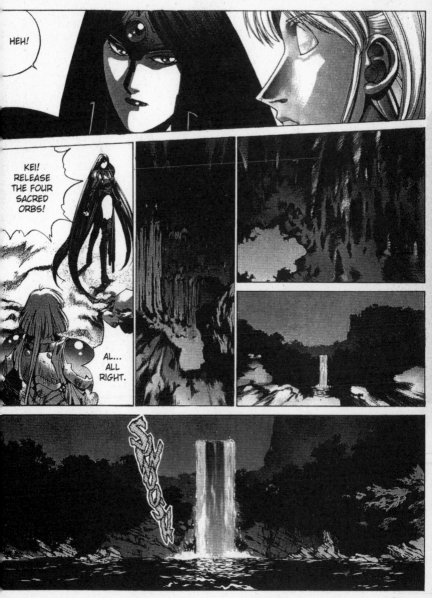

ORBS OF EARTH, WATER, FIRE AND WIND!
COME TO ME! TO MY SIDE!
BE GONE FROM HERE!
I'VE CHANGED MY MIND!
YES!
HON! CRUSH THIS STATUE!

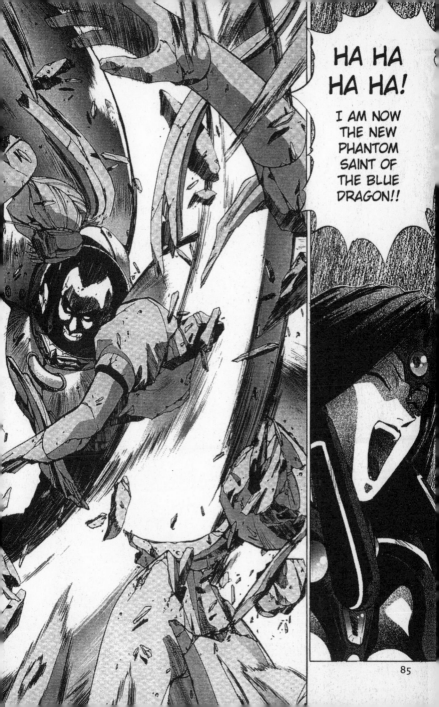

HA HA HA HA!

I AM NOW THE NEW PHANTOM SAINT OF THE BLUE DRAGON!!

BWASHH
SO LEEN, HOW DO YOU FEEL NOW?
DIS-APPOINT-ED, I BET. HA HA HA.
BUT I WAS EVEN MORE DIS-APPOINT-ED--
--AND HURT THAN YOU'LL EVER KNOW.
HA HA HA HA HA HA HA HA HA!
HEH HEH HEH HEH HEH HEH.

LEEN-
SAMA!

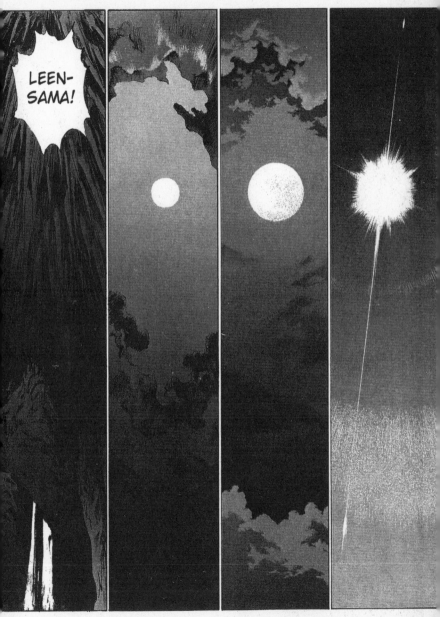

BLUE DRAGON PALACE.
WHY?!

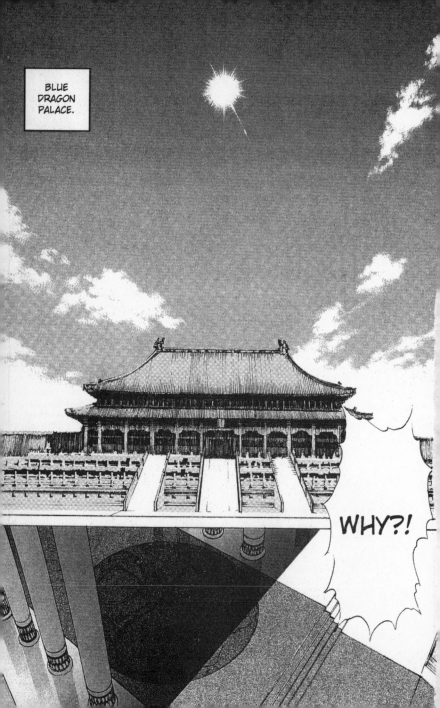

TELL ME, MEI-SAMA!
WHY AM I NOT THE NEXT PHANTOM SAINT?!
WHY LEEN?!
YOU DON'T KNOW WHY, NIE?
I DON'T UNDER-STAND!! WHY?!
I KNOW I AM STRONGER AND MORE SKILLED THAN LEEN!
I'LL NEVER UNDER-STAND!
MEI-SAMA, PLEASE EXPLAIN THE REASON TO ME.

IF YOU DON'T UNDERSTAND THE REASON WHY LEEN WAS CHOOSEN AS THE NEXT PHANTOM SAINT...
WELL, NIE, THAT IS THE REASON YOU WERE NOT CHOSEN.
WHAT?
LISTEN TO ME, NIE. I KNOW YOU ARE STRONGER AND MORE SKILLED THAN LEEN, BUT LEEN POSSESSES OTHER QUALITIES THAT YOU DO NOT.
THAT IS WHY I HAVE CHOSEN LEEN TO BE THE NEXT PHANTOM SAINT. FOR SHE HAS WHAT YOU DO NOT...
AND AS LONG AS YOU DO NOT UNDERSTAND WHY, YOU WILL NEVER BE PHANTOM SAINT OF THE BLUE DRAGON, EVEN IF YOU CAN MOVE HEAVEN AND EARTH.
BUT ...

NIE, YOU WILL REMAIN ONE OF THE TWELVE WARRIORS OF THE DIVINE DRAGON, AS YOU ARE NOW.
SWEAR ALLEGIANCE TO LEEN AND USE YOUR POWERS ON HER BEHALF.
DO YOU UNDER-STAND?
YES.
NO...
NOT LEEN...
NO...
NOT LEEN...
I AM THE PHANTOM SAINT OF THE BLUE DRAGON!
I AM!

SO NOW, I AM--
--THE PHANTOM SAINT OF THE BLUE DRAGON!
YES SIR!

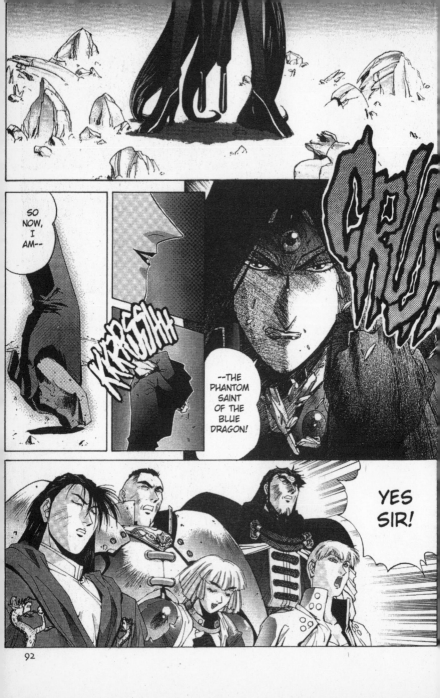

HOW DO YOU FEEL NOW THAT YOU GOT YOUR WISH, NIE? NOW THAT YOU'RE A PHANTOM SAINT?
THAT VOICE...
!!
HEH HEH HEH. I GUESS THOSE SACRED ORBS HAVE ACCEPTED YOU AS THE PHANTOM SAINT.
SPOK
SPOK
YOU'VE DONE WELL, NIE. ALL THE TROUBLE YOU WENT THROUGH TO TRICK LEEN HAS PAID OFF.
I AM TRULY GRATEFUL FOR YOUR ASSISTANCE...
WITHOUT YOUR HELP, I COULD NEVER HAVE BECOME THE PHANTOM SAINT.

I AM IN YOUR DEBT, SHIKI-SAMA.

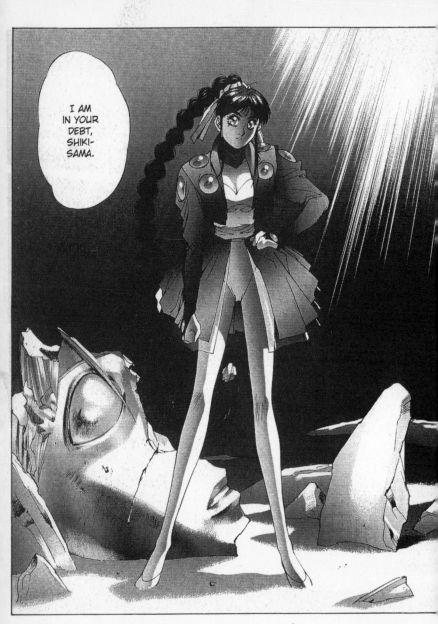

SHH
RR
AAA
SHH

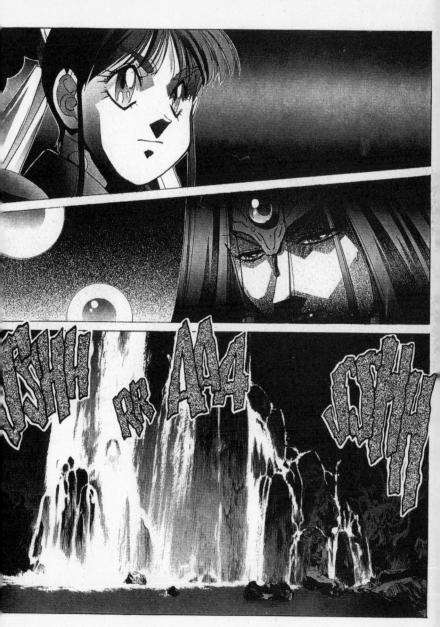

HA HA HA!
IT TICKLES.
WHAT SHOULD I DO? I NOW HAVE THE ORBS--
--AND NO ONE CAN STAND AGAINST ME!
...
DON'T CALL ME BY THAT NAME, NIE.
I'M SORRY!
SSSSHHH
EVEN COMPARED TO THIS PERSON STANDING BEFORE ME--
--I AM STONGER!

WHAT'S WRONG, NIE?
WHAT?!
PLINK
I AM NIE...
WITH YOUR HELP I BECAME THE PHANTOM SAINT OF THE BLUE DRAGON.
I WOULD LIKE TO SHOW YOU THE EXTENT OF MY APPRECIATION.
REALLY? AND HOW WILL YOU DO THAT?
YES!
GAZE
HERE.

HA HA HA HA HA HA HA
HA HA HA HA HA HA HA HA
HA HA HA HA
HA HA HA HA HA HA HA HA
HA HA HA HA HA HA HA HA
HA HA HA HA HA HA HA
HA HA HA HA HA HA HA HA HA

KRA-KOOM
BWOOOM
BWASH
HA HA HA. NICE, RAN! WE SHALL NOW TAKE OUR LEAVE. THIS PLACE SHALL CRUMBLE APART! YOU ALL GO ON AHEAD!
YES, SIR!
THESE FOUR ORBS ARE POWERFUL INDEED! LOOK WHAT I'VE DONE WITH JUST A FRACTION OF THEIR POWER!

HA HA HA HA. SOON, WITH THIS POWER, I SHALL RULE ALL FOUR TERRITORIES!

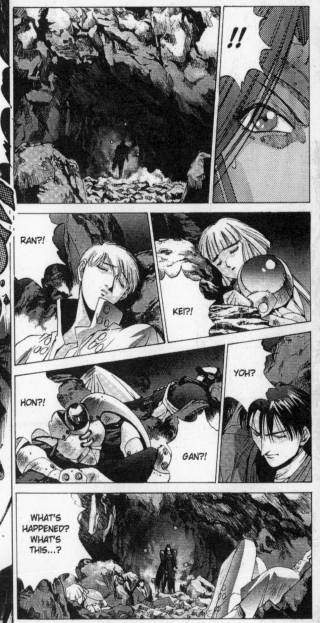

!!

RAN?!

KEI?!

HON?!

YOH?

GAN?!

WHAT'S HAPPENED? WHAT'S THIS...?

IT'S NOTHING REALLY.
!!
GASP!
NIE, I'M GOING TO TEACH YOU ONE THING.
ANYONE WHO HAS EVER GOTTEN ME ANGRY IS DEAD!
VWAAA
SSSHH
I AM DEL-PHINA!
!!

HA HA HA. YOU'LL REGRET THIS, NIE!
I AM THE STRONGEST NOW. NO ONE CAN BEAT ME--
--AS LONG AS I HAVE THE FOUR ORBS.
I UNDERSTAND, NIE!

AAAAHH...
UGHH!
BURN MY TRUE FORM INTO YOUR EYES AND GET READY TO GO TO HELL!

KRA-KASSHH
FWOOOSH
SHOOOSH
HEH HEH
HEH HEH!

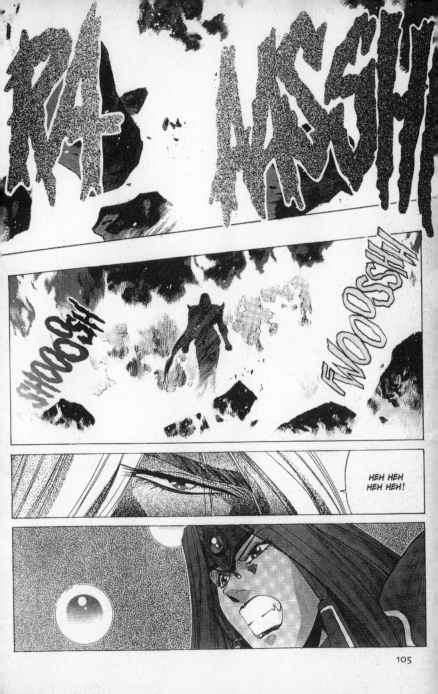

NIE, ARE YOU TRULY READY FOR THIS?
EVEN BEGGING FOR MERCY WON'T HELP YOU NOW.
HMPH! I WILL NEVER BEG FOR MERCY!
I AM NOW THE PHANTOM SAINT OF THE BLUE DRAGON, RULER OF TOI, ONE OF THE FOUR TERRITORIES!
WHOO OOSH
I WILL NOT LOSE!!
THEN LET'S SEE JUST WHAT KIND OF POWER YOU'VE GOT, PHANTOM SAINT.
OTHERWISE MY COMING ALL THE WAY TO THIS REMOTE LAND WILL HAVE BEEN FOR NOTHING.

I WILL NOT DISAPPOINT MY RULER, TYPHON-SAMA. HA HA HA.
SSSSHHH
FFF
YOU MEAN I'M...
RAN! YOH! GAN! WAKE UP! GET UP!
UGHH!
WHOOOOSSHH
SHHH
HAVE YOU FINALLY FIGURED IT OUT?
YOU'RE PRETTY SLOW!
SHHH
SHHH
THIS IS...
WHAT'S... WHAT'S THE MEANING OF THIS?

TOK
TOK
RAN?
SPOK
ISN'T THAT RAN?!
HEY, RAN! RAN!!
UHH...
WHERE'S LEEN-SAMA?
UHH...
LEEN-SAMA!!
RAN!

CHAO!!
GET IT TOGETHER, RAN! WHERE ARE LEEN-SAMA AND SHIKI?
HUH...
CLUTCH
CHAO! IT'S A TRAP! THE OTHER TWELVE WARRIORS OF THE DIVINE DRAGON...
GAN AND YOH AND EVEN SHIKI, THEY'RE TRYING TO KILL LEEN-SAMA!
HUH?
HUH?
GAN AND YOH?
YES... THEY...

WHAT'S THIS? WHAT'S GOING ON?
THESE HUMAN-SHAPED ROCKS...
THESE CAN'T BE...?
...
THAT'S EXACT-LY WHAT THEY ARE.
THE TWELVE WARRIORS OF THE DIVINE DRAGON WHO AIDED YOU WERE ACTUALLY NOTHING MORE THAN GOLEMS I CREATED.
I CREATED THEM WITH KNOWLEDGE I GLEANED FROM YOUR MEMORIES.

YOU...YOU PLANNED THIS ALL ALONG, DIDN'T YOU, DELPHINA?!!
HA!
LOOK WHO'S TALKING!
DIDN'T YOU DO THE SAME THING?
WHAT?!
WHAT'S WRONG, NIE? BACKING OFF? ARE YOU REALLY THAT SHOCKED?!
FAKE STONE WARRIORS WITH POWERS EQUAL TO THEIR REAL COUNTER-PARTS KILLED YOUR LEEN, THE NOW FORMER PHANTOM SAINT.
ARE YOU AFRAID OF THE POWER OF DELPHINA, THE GREEK SPECTER GOD?
NIE!

ZWOOSH!
WHAT?!
YOU!!
UGGH!
I'LL DESTROY YOU, NIE!
HA HA HA HA HA!
I NOW UNDERSTAND THE POWERS OF THE PEOPLE IN THIS LAND.
I THINK IT WOULD BE ACTUALLY RATHER EASY TO CONQUER.

DELPHINA! I'M GOING TO SHOW YOU THE EXTENT OF MY POWER! THE POWER OF ONE OF THE BLUE DRAGON!!
DARK RISING WAVES OF THE BLACK DRAGON!!

YEARGH!!
!?
HMPH! IS THAT IT?

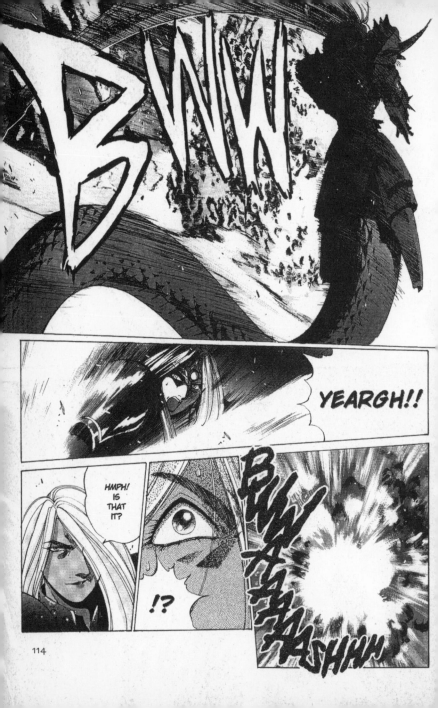

SHRAKK
NOOOO!
THIS CAN'T...?!
UGH!
AHH... AHH...
SLITHER
SLITHER

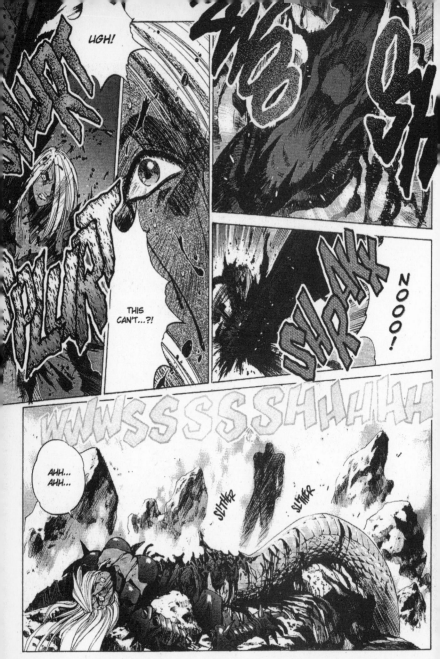

I DON'T KNOW MUCH ABOUT THE WESTERN WORLD BUT...
HA! SOME GREEK SPECTER GOD YOU ARE!
I WILL SOON RULE THESE LANDS!
THERE IS NO MATCH FOR ME, THE BLACK DRAGON!
HA HA HA HA HA HA HA HA!
THEN I SHALL GO CONQUER THE WORLD CALLED GREECE!
AGH!

THIS CAN'T BE! I JUST...
I DON'T THINK THAT WILL BE POSSIBLE.
HOW STUPID YOU TRULY ARE! YOU DIDN'T THINK I COULD DUPLICATE MYSELF AS WELL?!
THE ONE YOU KILLED IS JUST ANOTHER GOLEM I CREATED.
SPURT
GAAK!!
THWUMP

HEH HEH. WHAT A WEAK WO- MAN...
SHUT YOUR MOUTH! I STILL CONTROL THE FOUR ORBS.
THEY'LL HEAL THIS WOUND...
THE FOUR ORBS? AND JUST WHERE ARE THEY?
WHOOOSH
THEY TIRED OF YOU WHEN THEY SAW JUST HOW WEAK YOU TRULY ARE.
IT... CAN'T...
WHAP
HA HA HA. IS THIS THE POWER OF THE PHANTOM SAINT OF THE BLUE DRAGON? IT DOESN'T EVEN MAKE FOR AN INTERESTING TALE.
I SHALL RETURN TO GREECE AND REPORT TO TYPHON-SAMA THAT THE PEOPLE HERE ARE...
TELL HIM THERE IS ONE MIGHTY WAR- RIOR!
WHO?!

HHHHHH!

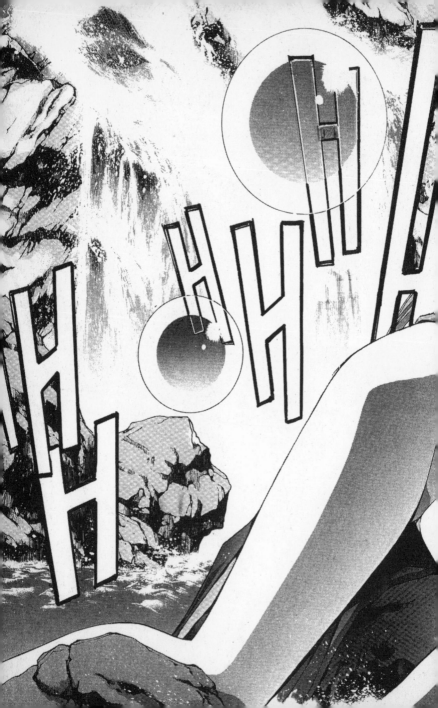

Y... YOU...
FTHUSHHH
SPLOOSH
FWWOOSH!
LEEN?!

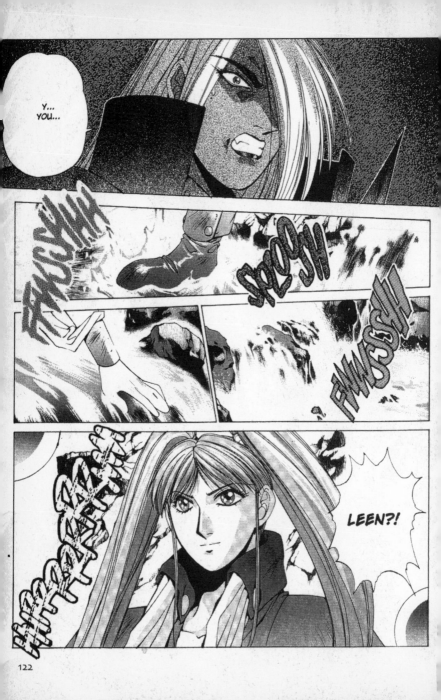

KWWOO OOOO SH
WHY... WHY... WHY ARE YOU HERE? YOU'RE ALIVE?!
DELPHINA OF GREECE, WASN'T IT?
IT'S TIME TO PUT AN END TO BOTH YOUR SCHEMING.
HOW? NIE BROKE YOU INTO LITTLE PIECES!
SHE'S... ALIVE?!
LEEN...?
WHILE I WAS TRAPPED IN THE WATER CHAMBER, I DIFFUSED MYSELF INTO FOUR ENTITIES AND TRANSFERRED THEM INTO THE FOUR ORBS.
JUST LIKE YOU, I USED A FAKE DOUBLE OF MYSELF.

I THEN RE-CREATED MY BODY WITH WATER.
I COULD HAVE FREED MYSELF FROM THE WATER CHAMBER, BUT...
I WANTED TO FIND OUT JUST WHO WAS ACTUALLY BEHIND ALL THIS.
NO!
WHEN THE ORBS WERE TRAPPED IN THE WATER CHAMBER, I WAS A BIT WORRIED--
--AS TO WHETHER I WOULD BE ABLE TO RE-ESTABLISH MY TRUE FORM.
I'M HERE NOW BECAUSE NIE RELEASED THE FOUR ORBS.
ARGH... LEEN...
IS THAT IT? HA HA. IS THAT WHAT HAPPENED?
LEEN... HA HA HA.

LEEN...
WHEN WAS IT?
WHEN DID YOU DISCOVER MY PLAN?
NIE...
WHUMP
AFTER THE SHIP WENT DOWN, I WAS TOLD OF YOUR DECEPTION BY THE REAL SHIKI.

UNFORTUNATELY, I'M UNABLE TO LOCATE THE KEY TO FINDING THE ORB OF GOLD THIS TIME, BUT...

...AND THAT'S WHAT'S GOING ON.

PFOOSH

CHINK!

UGGH!!

PRFSSSH

WHAT THE...?!

NO MORE USING GOLEMS--

--AS LONG AS THESE FOUR ORBS ARE WATCHING.

FTFWMS SSS SFFSHH HHH

THAT'S JUST GREAT, LEEN.
YOU'RE WELCOME.
SHHRAASH
FSSSHH
W HOOOOO OOOSSHH

NOW, THE TIME FOR EXPLANATIONS IS OVER.
I UNDERSTAND. SHOW ME YOUR POWER!
FEEL THE POWER OF THE ONE TRUE PHANTOM SAINT OF THE BLUE DRAGON!
OR WHAT YOU BELIEVE TO BE POWER, LEEN.

FHWOOOOOO

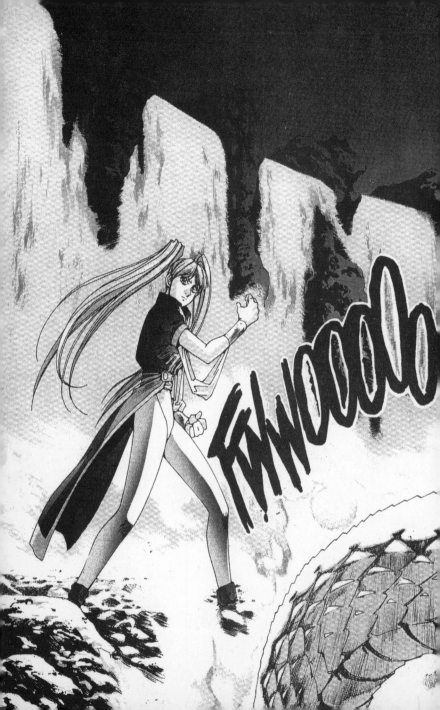

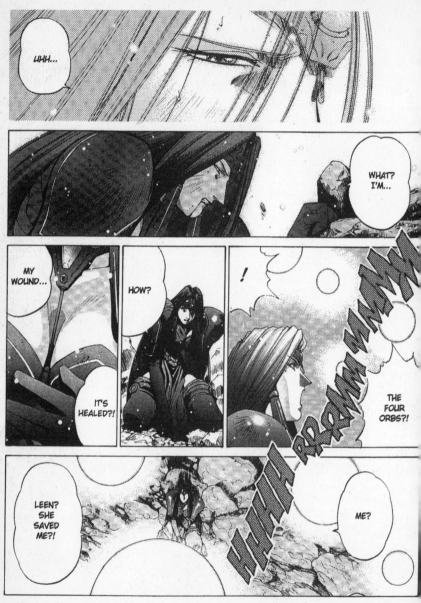

UHH...

WHAT?
I'M...

MY
WOUND...

HOW?

!

THE
FOUR
ORBS?!

IT'S
HEALED?!

LEEN?
SHE
SAVED
ME?!

ME?

REARGH!
HIYAAA!
SHII–INK

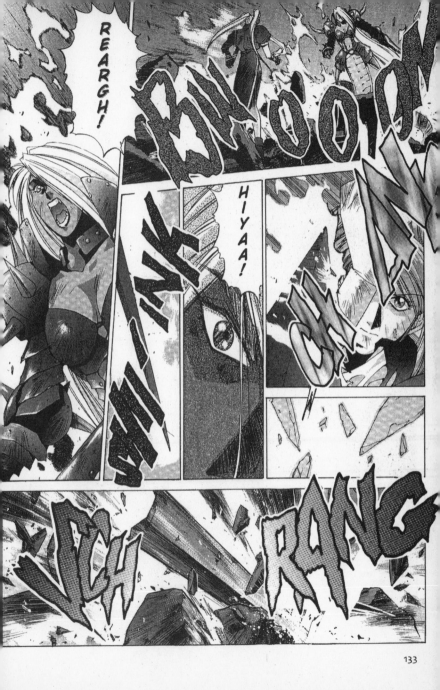

DRAGON WATER BLAST!
WHAT?!
UGGH!

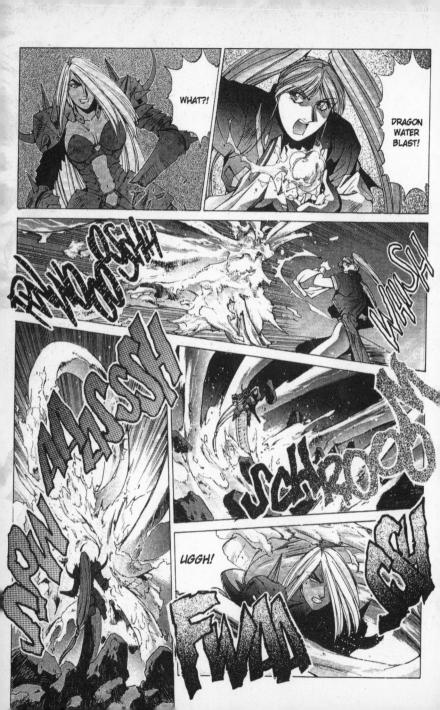

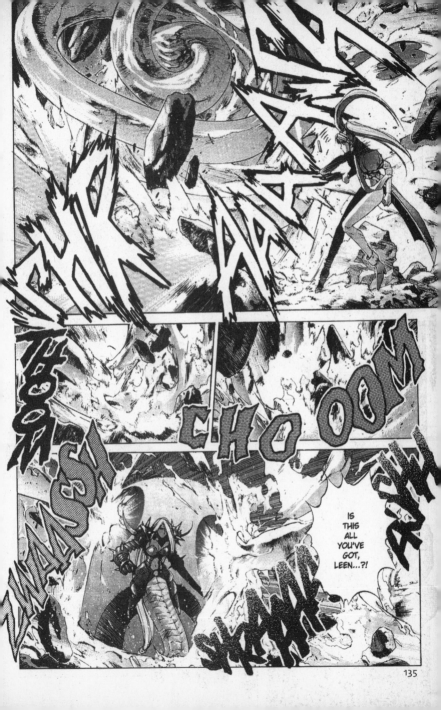

IS THIS ALL YOU'VE GOT, LEEN...?!

135

WHAT'S HAPPEN-ING?!
ARRGGH!
LEEN!!

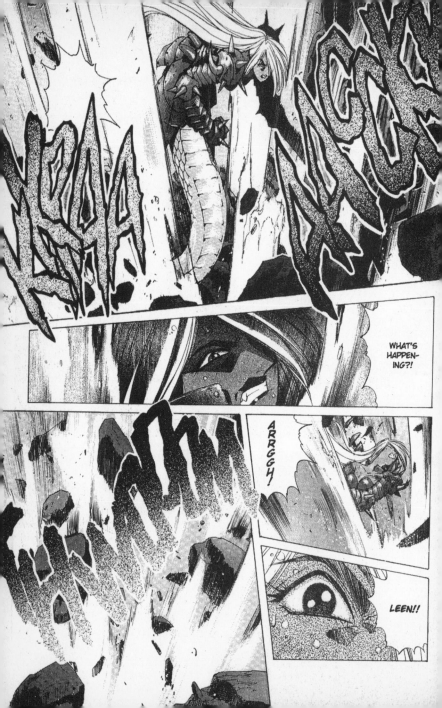

THERE IS NO ESCAPING MY DRAGON WATER BLAST! ARE YOU READY?
DRAGON HEAVEN'S CHAIN!!
FEEL THE DRAGON GOD'S ROAR AS LIGHT AND WATER EXPLODE!
SACRED ORBS, RETURN TO ME!

UGGH!
NI... NIE?!
HUFF!
HUFF!
HUFF!
HUFF!
THUD!
UMPH!

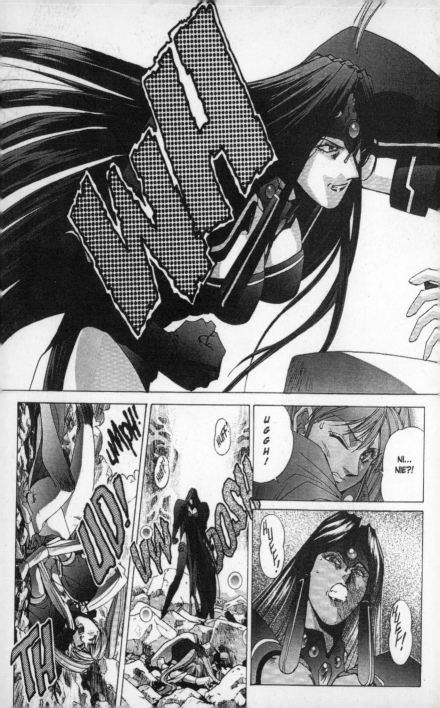

I WAS DOWN, BUT FAR FROM OUT. I DID NOT NEED YOUR HELP.
LEEN, I DON'T NEED YOUR SYMPATHY!

YOU DARED TO PRESUME I, NIE, NEEDED YOUR HELP?! DON'T MAKE ME LAUGH!
YOU! DON'T BE SO SELF-RIGHTEOUS! WHO DO YOU THINK I AM?

NIE...
NOW'S MY CHANCE. THE WATER HAS LET UP.
DIE, LEEN!! RE-MEMBER MY POWER!
I AM NIE, THE BLACK DRAGON! NIE, THE TRUE PHANTOM SAINT OF THE BLUE DRAGON!

!!
ALWAYS GETTING IN THE WAY. WHEN WILL YOU SHUT UP?!
DEL... DEL-PHINA!!
GILGAMESH!

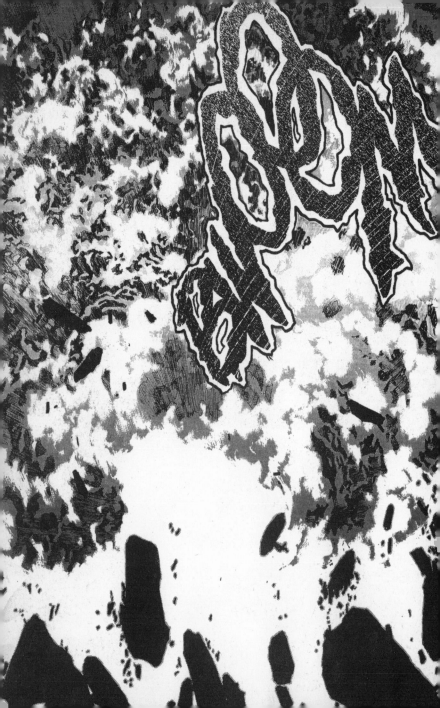

FFWMSSS
THOOM
FWOOO

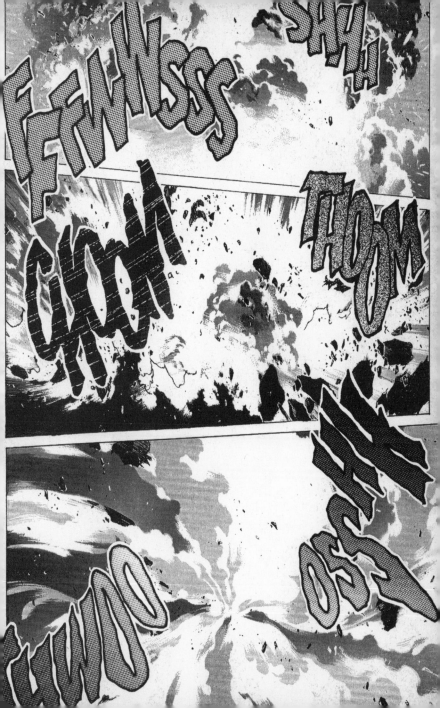

LEEN!
NIE!
YAAHH!!

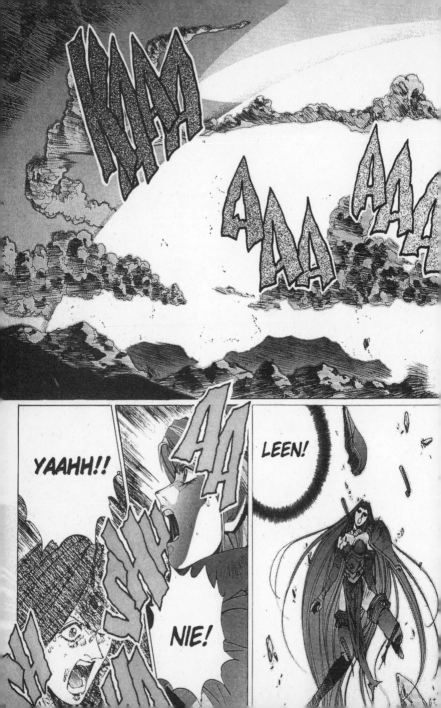

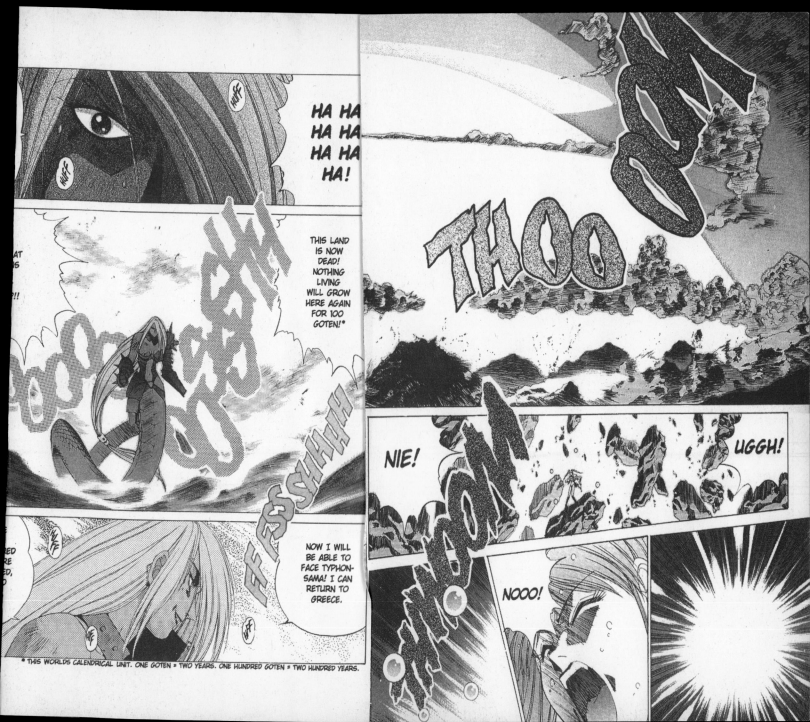

HA HA HA HA HA HA HA!

THIS LAND IS NOW DEAD! NOTHING LIVING WILL GROW HERE AGAIN FOR 100 GOTEN!*

NOW I WILL BE ABLE TO FACE TYPHON-SAMA! I CAN RETURN TO GREECE.

* THIS WORLD'S CALENDRICAL UNIT. ONE GOTEN = TWO YEARS. ONE HUNDRED GOTEN = TWO HUNDRED YEARS.

THOO

NIE!

UGGH!

NOOO!

HA HA HA HA!
SEE WH HAPPEN WHEN I GE ANGRY
LEEN, NI AND THE FOUR SAC ORBS WE INCINERAT BUT I N LONGER CARE!

!!
NO!
LEEN-SAMA...
THAT LIGHT...
QUICKLY! WE SHOULD BE AT LEEN-SAMA'S SIDE!
HURRY!
OOOOSHHH

NO! IMPOSSIBLE! NO ONE COULD HAVE LIVED THROUGH IT!
HUFF
HUFF
NO ONE!
WHAT?! WHO...?!
SOMEONE SURVIVED MY GILGAMESH SPELL?
THAT'S NOT GOING TO HAPPEN!
THE CRYING OF THE GRASS, THE TREES, THE VOICE OF NATURE...
CAN YOU HEAR THEM?

I CAN HEAR THEM! I CAN HEAR THE SCREAMS OF THE SOULS OF ALL THOSE WHO DIED IN YOUR BLAST.
!

IN TRYING TO KILL US, YOU TOOK THOUSANDS UPON THOUSANDS OF LIVES. THE SPIRITS, THE ANIMALS, THE GRASS, THE TREES, THE FOREST...
THERE IS NO MERCY FOR YOU!

N...
NO...
NOOO!!
WITH ALL MY BODY, ALL MY SOUL, I'M GOING TO--
--KILL YOU!!
HELP ME!!
HELP ME, TYPHON-SAMA!!
SACRED BLUE DRAGON TRANS-FORM-ATION!

ARRGH!!

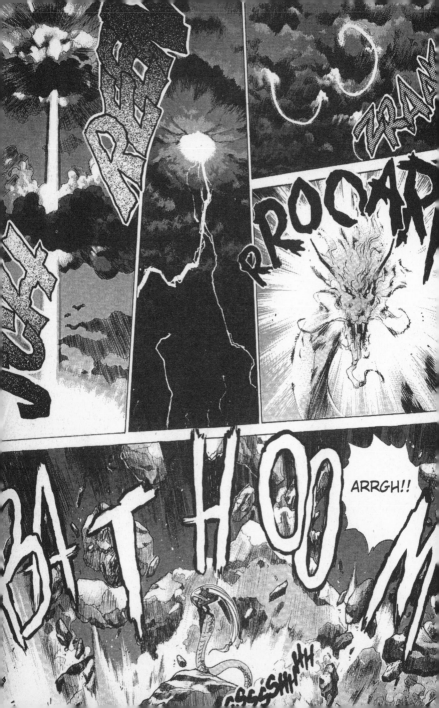

THAT?!
CHATTER CHATTER
IS THAT LEEN'S TRUE FORM?!
THAT!!
WHOOOOOOSSSH

FWOOOO
KRSH
KRRRSH
KRSH
ZZRRAAAAGSH!!

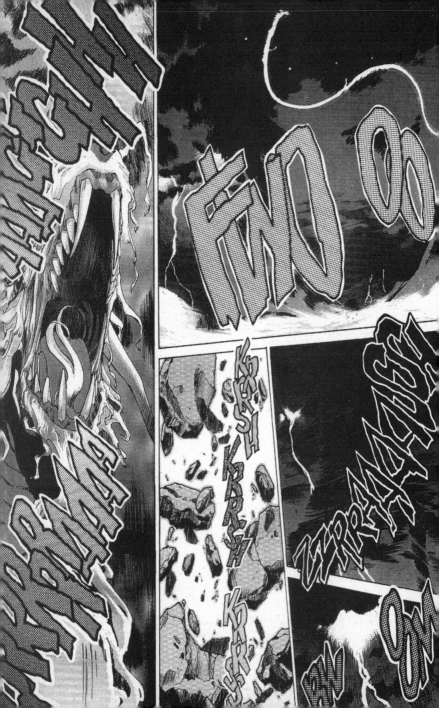

WHAT IS ALL THIS?
EVERYTHING IS TURNING ON ME. THE HOSTILITY IS DIRECTED SOLELY AT ME.
THAT'S IT! THE HEAVENS, THE EARTH, EVEN THE AIR...!
THEY'RE ALL CALLING FOR MY DEATH!
CAN THIS... CAN THIS...
CAN THIS BE HAPPENING?

FWOOOOOSH
TYPHON-SAMA!!
PLEASE SAVE ME!!!
TYPHON-SAMA!!!
VWAASHHH

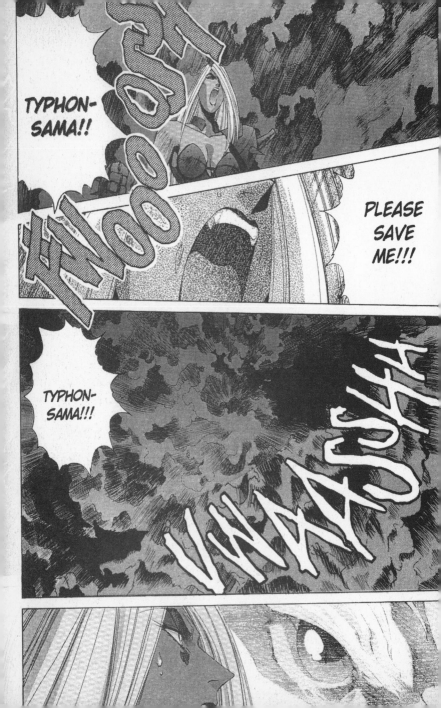

!!
TYPHON-SAMA!
YEAARGGHH!

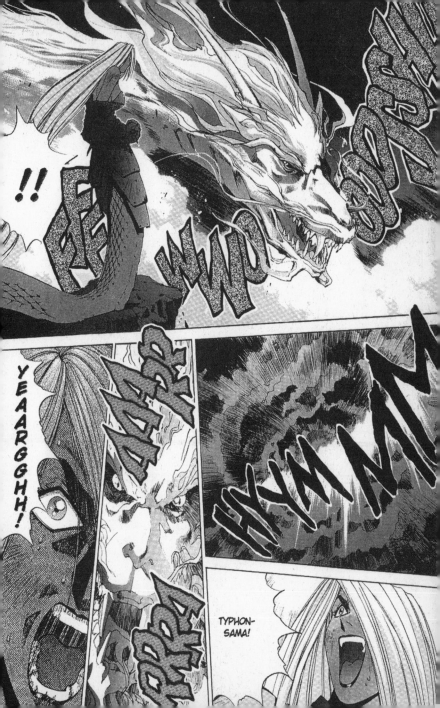

WHAT...

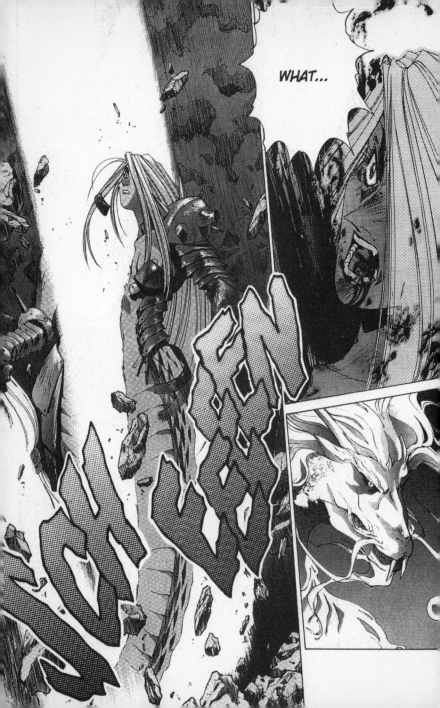

AHH...
YAAAAAH!
WASHH
...

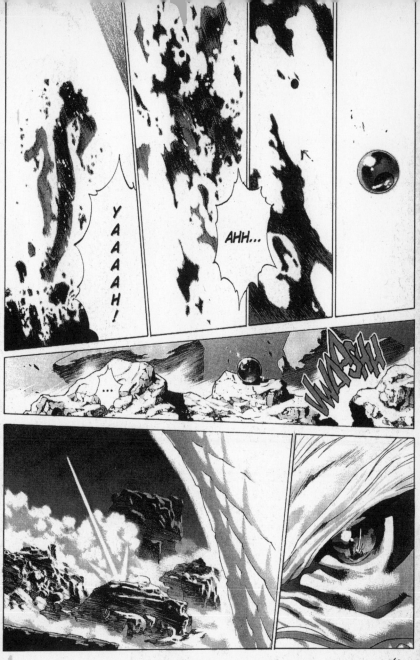

THIS IS THE FIRST TIME I HAVE LAID EYES UPON YOU, LEEN, RULER OF TOI, PHANTOM SAINT OF THE BLUE DRAGON.
FIRST, I MUST OFFER MY APOLOGIES.
I AM SORRY FOR THE LITTLE SNAKE I SENT INTO YOUR LAND'S GRASS.
FWWOOOO
LEEN, I LOOK FORWARD TO SEEING YOU AGAIN. UNTIL THEN, PLEASE TAKE CARE OF YOURSELF.
I MUST ALSO BE GOING. BACK TO GREECE...
NEXT TIME, I WILL SEND SOMEONE WHO WILL BE MORE OF A CHALLENGE FOR YOU.
LEEN OF THE BLUE DRAGON... HA HA HA.

OO OSSHH
I HOPE YOU WILL FORGIVE ME THIS TIME.
I WANT TO BE ABLE TO ENJOY OUR NEXT ENCOUNTER.
HWO OOO OSSH
HA HA HA HA HA HA HA HA!

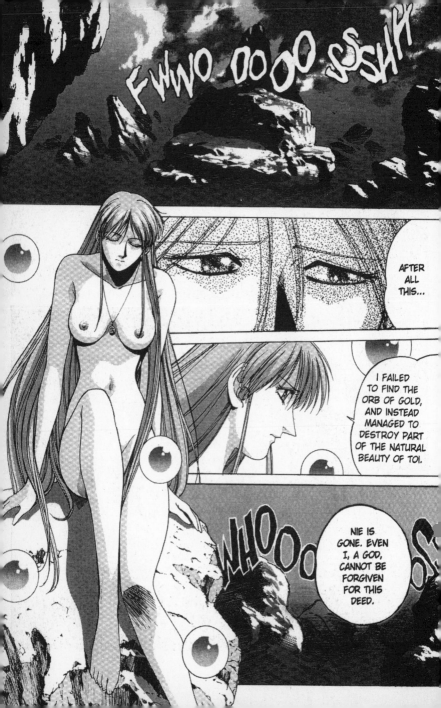

FWWO OOOO SSSH

AFTER ALL THIS...

I FAILED TO FIND THE ORB OF GOLD, AND INSTEAD MANAGED TO DESTROY PART OF THE NATURAL BEAUTY OF TOI.

WHOOO OOOS

NIE IS GONE. EVEN I, A GOD, CANNOT BE FORGIVEN FOR THIS DEED.

I AM...
LEEN-SAMA!!
HOW CAN I ATONE FOR THIS DISASTER?
HWWISSSHH
FWOOOO OO SSH
TOK
TOK
TOK
TOK

SHOOSH
LEEN-SAMA!
TOK TOK TOK
AH!
AH!
LEEN-SAMA! WE SAW A BLUE DRAGON IN HE SKY AND WERE WONDERING...
GAN! LOOK THE OTHER WAY!
HEH HEH. IT'S ALL RIGHT! THERE'S NO HARM IN LOOKING.
A LOOK WON'T KILL ME.
TOK
AS FOR NATURE HERE...
HWOOOOOOSH
HOW MANY GOTEN WILL IT BE BEFORE THIS PLACE RETURNS TO THE WAY IT ONCE WAS?

KWOOOSHH
EVEN THOUGH THE SUN BEGINS TO RISE...
NIE...
AND THE PEOPLE BACK AT THE PALACE ARE AWAITING OUR RETURN.
WE MUST PRAY FOR THOSE WHO DIED IN THIS BATTLE.
WELL, NOW... LET US GET BACK TO THE PALACE.
YES, SIR!
BOW

UHHH...

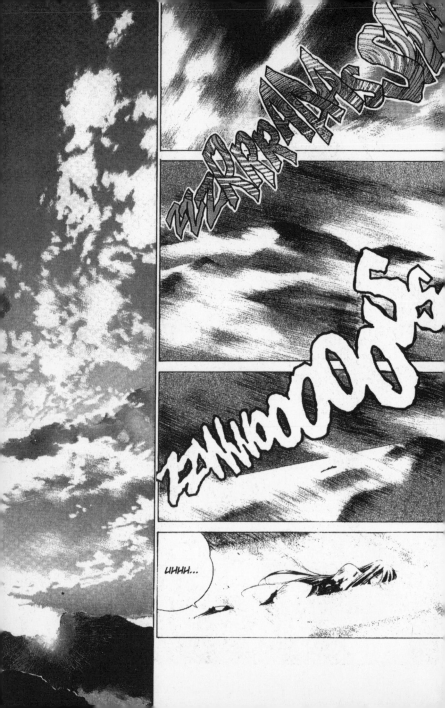

...POWER...
HWWOO OO OOSHH
I...I HATE LEEN! I RESENT HER...
I WANT MORE...
SSHH
KRS
MORE...
FWOOOO OOSSHH
POWER!
IF I HAD MORE POWER...
WHAT?
IS THAT SO? DO YOU REALLY DESIRE SUCH POWER?

TREMEN-DOUS POWER!
IF YOU WANT IT, I SHALL GIVE IT TO YOU.
COME WITH ME!
FW OOO
The End.

ABOUT KIA ASAMIYA

Kia Asamiya is a world-famous master of manga. He has created several series, including *Silent Mobius, Dark Angel, Gunhed* and *Nadesico*, which have been the basis for many popular motion pictures and anime. His titles define entire genres within Japanese popular culture and he is respected by fans and creators alike.

A fan of American comic books, he has done manga adaptations of *Star Wars*, and was the artist for *Uncanny X-Men* and *Batman: Child of Dreams*.

A frequent visitor to the United States and a popular American convention guest, he is the founder of his own manga workshop, Studio Tron.

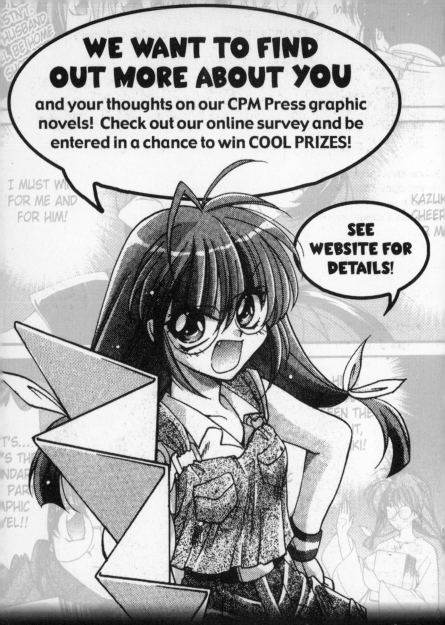

www.cpmpress.com/survey/